10
TIME-SAVING
TIPS FOR
BUSY PARENTS

10
TIME-SAVING
TIPS FOR
BUSY PARENTS

DR. MAGDALENA BATTLES

WHITAKER
HOUSE

10 Time-Saving Tips for Busy Parents

Dr. Magdalena Battles
DrErinMagdalena@hotmail.com
www.LivingJoyDaily.com

ISBN: 978-1-64123-592-1
eBook ISBN: 978-1-64123-593-8
Printed in the United States of America
© 2021 by Magdalena Battles

Whitaker House
1030 Hunt Valley Circle
New Kensington, PA 15068
www.whitakerhouse.com

Library of Congress Cataloging-in-Publication Data (Pending)

1 2 3 4 5 6 7 8 9 10 11 **LU** 28 27 26 25 24 23 22 21

CONTENTS

INTRODUCTION:
LEAVING A LEGACY OF TIME WELL SPENT

I want to leave this world feeling confident of having made a difference. We all want to leave a legacy of some kind, and our legacy depends wholly on the choices we make and the way we spend our time. If we want to make a positive impact on the world, then we must manage our time in such a way that maximizes our efforts toward our desired impact. For many of us, myself included, the most important impact of all is the one we leave on the people we love. Therefore, spending quality time with them is more than just important; it is necessary. Being able to accomplish our tasks effectively and efficiently gives us more time to spend with our loved ones.

I am often asked, "How do you do it all?" or "How do you get everything done?" I don't say this to brag, because I am not a perfect mom, nor am I "Super-Mom." But other people have noticed that I get a lot done in any given day. The reason for my productivity is good time management. Using time management to be more successful at home, and to experience less stress in every area of life, is attainable for every parent. What mom couldn't benefit from finding a few more minutes—or maybe even a few more hours—throughout the day to do what she wants?

My desire is to share some tips and tricks to help other moms experience the joy of getting to church before it starts; having time to spend with their book club, cake club, or wine club; and to experience mornings that aren't harried, rushed, and insane.

My husband and I have three small children: an eight-year-old daughter and six-year-old twin boys. The time management tips I'm about to share have been working for our family since before our children were born. Effective time management became even more crucial once they came along. The time management tips I outline in this book work for our family and help us feel like our life and our household are under control, even when so much around us is out of our control.

While I can't guarantee that every tip will work for you, you should be able to find at least a few tricks that will benefit you and your household. You can gain more control over your weeks and days when you begin to apply some of the tips from this book to your own life. You can start today, but it is up to *you* to make the decision regarding changes you must make in the time management of your household.

When you feel in control of your time management—rather than feeling as if your schedule is out of your control—you become a happier person, parent, and spouse. Your kids appreciate and thrive from the structure you create by effectively applying time management skills, and you will find yourself accomplishing more so that you have extra time to spend with your spouse and children.

 WHEN YOU FEEL IN CONTROL OF YOUR TIME MANAGEMENT, YOU BECOME A HAPPIER PERSON, PARENT, AND SPOUSE.

Through the application of the tips I am about to share, your family members will become more actively involved in the tasks required to run a household. You don't need to be the parent who "does it all." You need to be a parent who knows when to say no, knows how to delegate, and gets the family involved in keeping the household running.

Get excited! Your life is about to get easier, because when you practice optimal time management, you become better organized, more productive, and, consequently, less stressed (and more joyful). None of us is perfect, so please don't expect this book to instruct you on becoming a perfect parent or spouse. There are days when I get off track and my to-do list doesn't get done or dinner doesn't get made; but, as a whole, I implement these tips on such a regular basis, and have utilized them for so long, that they have become habits. Applying these tips will enable you to create better time management habits so that your household runs more smoothly and your family is as productive and fulfilled as possible.

This book is based on my popular article from Lifehack.org entitled "10 Time Management Tips Every Busy Parent Needs to Know." Each chapter expounds in greater detail on one of these ten tips, providing more pointed guidance and personal stories to help you better apply these time management principles to your own life—starting today! Organizing your home is a great accomplishment, but what about organizing your life? Time management is the best way to start organizing your life and purging any activities that don't bring you joy, so that you have enough time to pursue those things that do.

CHAPTER I:

KNOW YOUR HIERARCHY OF IMPORTANCE

What is most important to you in this life? Is it your job? Is it your family? Is it your relationship with God? It is imperative that *you* know what is most important in your life and the life of your family. If you don't have your priorities in order, how can you ever say no to anything? When you haven't clearly defined what is most important, then your time tends to be spent anywhere and everywhere without a plan. But once you know what is most important in your life, you can then filter your decisions, such as those regarding the activities you pursue, through a lens that asks, "How does this affect what is most important in my life?"

SAYING NO

When we recognize and clearly define what we value, we can start saying no to activities and decisions that don't align with our values. Being able to say no is beneficial, because it allows us to say yes to the things that *do* matter to us. If we don't have clearly defined values, we don't know when we ought to say no. Saying no becomes easier when our values are clearly defined.

In my family, we place a high value on our community. We love where we live, in the suburbs between the cities of Dallas and Fort Worth, Texas. This suburban area appeals to us because it feels like a small town, yet we have easy access to city amenities. Our church, our children's schools, sports fields, grocery stores, and everything else that we need is within a ten-mile radius of our home. What makes this place especially valuable to us are the people and the sense of community. People help their neighbors and gladly go the extra mile for others. And when it comes to the circles of friends we have formed here, we think of them as family.

 ONCE YOU KNOW WHAT IS MOST IMPORTANT IN YOUR LIFE, YOU CAN FILTER YOUR DECISIONS THROUGH THAT LENS.

My husband and I have facilitated a couples' Bible study, and I led a weekly women's Bible study in our home for three years. I have served on a variety of boards within the community, including a "moms of multiples" group and our HOA. I started a book club for moms in our community, and I prioritize volunteering at my kids' schools. The relationships we've forged in our community—at church, in our neighborhood, in the schools, in various activities—fill us with joy. We chose our community and our activities with great intentionality. Why do I tell you all of this? Because it explains why we aren't willing to move, even if my husband could earn more money elsewhere. In fact, he has been offered jobs with higher salaries, but he's turned them down because accepting them would have entailed our moving away from our community.

Unless God leads us to move away, relocating is not an option for us. We won't do it, not for a million dollars. We believe God led us to this community because it is the best place for us to live and raise our kids. We want to be here. We value where we live more than money. Do thoughts of a bigger house or better vehicles or more money in the bank ever sway us? No amount of money or assets could ever equal the value we place on our community. Our conscious decision to rank our community above money in importance makes our decisions easy. The time that we spend in our community, serving and being involved in worthwhile activities, is the reason I consider community in the top five in my hierarchy of importance.

The same set of values governs the activities I choose to participate in. I am an involved parent, and I could easily sign up for more than I can handle because I enjoy volunteering and being plugged into my community. I regularly assess which activities and involvements align with *my* personal hierarchy of importance. My hierarchy is ordered as follows: God first, husband second, and kids third. If any of these priorities falls out of order as a result of my overextending myself or committing to an excessive number of activities, then my all-important relationships with God, my husband, and my kids fail. If I am not home due to an overscheduling of activities, then I will likely not have enough time or energy for meaningful conversations with my husband in the evenings; for tucking my kids into bed at night with stories, songs, and prayers; or for prayer and Bible study. If I commit to every activity that comes my way, then I definitely won't be able to keep up with what is actually most important in my life.

When you say yes to a particular activity, you are also saying no to something else, because you can't do it all. If you say yes to an invitation to join a new book club, you may be saying no to family dinner on the nights when that book club meets. If your priority is to have dinner with your family just about every night, then it may be that joining the book club is not an activity that aligns with your values.

You need to first determine your highest priorities—the people and things you value most. Then, when you are presented with an opportunity that would claim a portion of your time—what opportunity doesn't—then you will be better equipped to decide whether to accept or decline. It is far easier to say no to certain activities when you have clearly defined your top values. When you stay committed to those values, you will be a happier person and a better spouse and parent in the long run. If you are constantly saying yes to every opportunity that crosses your path, you will end up overscheduled, overworked, and spread too thin. Don't let this happen to you. Learn to say no!

 WHEN YOU SAY YES TO A PARTICULAR ACTIVITY, YOU ARE ALSO SAYING NO TO SOMETHING ELSE, BECAUSE YOU CAN'T DO IT ALL.

HOW TO DEVELOP YOUR HIERARCHY OF IMPORTANCE

In order to say no to activities that don't align with your values, you first need to define your hierarchy of importance. The following are significant questions to ask yourself. Take time to contemplate and reflect on your answers.

1. What is most important to you? What do you value most in this world?

2. Where is most of your time spent during the week (not counting sleeping)?

3. Where would you like to spend most of your time during the week?

4. What changes can you make so that your responses to #2 and #3 align more closely?

5. Can you list the five most important areas or people in your life?

6. Can you number those top five areas or people in order of importance from 1 to 5, with 1 being the most important?

Once you know what is most important in your life, you can better evaluate your activities by asking yourself: Which of my daily activities align with my hierarchy of importance? Which activities do not?

I spend a lot of time doing laundry. Now, laundry is not especially high on my hierarchy of importance, nor is it something I love doing. However, by doing laundry, I'm showing love to my husband and my children, numbers two and three in my hierarchy of importance. Providing my family with clean clothes and linens aligns with my values and the hierarchy of importance I have set for myself. In addition to laundry, I spend much of my days cleaning the house, preparing meals, and washing dishes. None of these activities is something I would ever call a hobby of mine. They aren't things I do because I particularly enjoy them. However, a high priority of mine is taking care of my family and the place where we live together. Therefore, any activities involved in caring for my family and our home are essential, and I need to work them into my weekly schedule. If I stretch myself too thin doing other things, then, when it comes time to get work done around the house, I may feel bitter, resentful, and overworked because I am out of time and energy. In order to keep caring for my family and home—a priority that falls within the top three items in my hierarchy of importance—I need to exercise care in the way I expend my personal resources of time and energy, so that they are not depleted.

Do your regular activities energize you or deplete you? Are you able to provide for the people who are most important to you, or do certain pastimes and pursuits impede your ability to be the spouse and parent you desire to be? Can you identify any activities that are not at the top of your hierarchy of importance, yet tend to deplete your time and energy throughout the week? Are there any changes you could make to reduce or eliminate certain activities in order to invest more time and energy in the people and pursuits that matter most to you?

 YOU AND YOUR FAMILY MEMBERS CAN'T FUNCTION AS A TEAM IF YOU AREN'T MOVING TOWARD THE SAME GOALS.

Your hierarchy of importance may resemble mine, but it is bound to be at least a little different. Determining your own hierarchy of importance is imperative because it equips you to decide which activities align with your priorities and which ones do not. You need to make that decision for yourself.

After determining your hierarchy of importance, the next step is defining your personal or family values and purpose. You and the other members of your household should be a team, and you can't function as a team if you aren't moving toward the same goals.

CREATE A FAMILY MISSION STATEMENT

One way that my family has clearly defined its purpose and values has been by creating a family mission statement. Most organizations, from corporations to nonprofits to churches, have a mission statement—a concise, memorable way of expressing clearly the purpose of the collective group. Increasingly, families are getting on the mission-statement bandwagon, as well. Creating a family mission statement can be a significant step in strengthening connections between yourself and your family members, helping you to function more as a team, and imparting a sense of shared purpose. Once you have crafted your family mission statement, you will be empowered to say no to activities and invitations that don't align with your family's purpose.

I am going to give you a crash course in family mission-statement planning, so you can simply and easily craft your own family mission statement this very week. Taking this step will help your family put into writing the purpose you have together, and the results will be amazing.

1. **Set up a meeting.** The first thing you will need to do is to meet as a family. Call a family meeting when you have at least an hour to sit down and talk together as an entire family. If you have kids who are grown and have already left the nest, that's okay. The focus of the meeting is for those currently living in the household. Make the atmosphere comfortable, so it's conducive to positive conversation and productive discussion. Consider meeting on the porch with lemonade and snacks if it's warm; in winter, you might cozy up beside the fireplace with

mugs of hot chocolate. You don't want your family members to view this activity as a punishment or an obligation. Instead, you want everyone to experience this meeting as a fun time of family bonding. Bring out some hot chocolate and cookies, and cozy up with some blankets near the fireplace.

2. **Brainstorm.** Once everyone is comfortably seated together, explain the exercise: as a family, you are going to brainstorm your family purpose. The sky is the limit! Everyone gets to offer input, even the youngest members of the family, provided they are old enough to understand the exercise and communicate their ideas. My twin sons were four years old when we held our family mission-statement planning session. I remember being amazed at their enthusiasm and at the number of valid suggestions they made that were included in our final statement. I started out by asking, simply, "What do you think is the purpose of our family?" Some of the answers my kids came up with were as follows: "To love God"; "To love each other"; "To have good manners." They also threw in some funny suggestions, but when we got down to the heart of each one, their ideas aligned with all the other values we wanted to include. For example, Alex suggested, as part of our purpose, "eating ice cream and pizza together." Sounds like a legitimate family purpose coming from a four-year-old. But what is eating ice cream and pizza together really about? For my four-year-old, and for the rest of us, it's about enjoying life together.

3. **Record and evaluate all suggestions.** Jot down all the suggestions from everyone, and be specific about identifying each family member's contributions. This will be important later on, because you will want to include suggestions from everyone in the finalized mission statement. At first glance, some suggestions may not seem as important as others, but it is vital

to give equal value to everyone's ideas. Be sure that everyone in the family provides at least one suggestion. For all family members to be on board with the final mission statement, they all need to be contributors. It's difficult to get your kids to find a mission statement meaningful, and worth the effort of aligning their lives with, if they had nothing to do with its creation. Participation from all family members, and the inclusion of at least one suggestion from each family member, is ideal.

4. **Select key statement(s) and finalize wording.** Once the list of suggestions is complete, the parents should form a mission statement, including as many or as few of the suggestions from the list as appropriate—again, ideally including at least one concept contributed from each family member. If you need to reword a statement or make it more generalized, do so, but explain your reasons when you present the finalized mission statement to your family. For example, our daughter, Brielle, who was six when we crafted our family statement, suggested that we not yell at each other or engage in name-calling. This idea translated into our mission statement as "loving one another as we love ourselves" and "speaking with kind words and tone of voice."

Our finalized mission statement was a total of ten declarations. Yours may be longer or shorter, depending on the ideas your family shares and the values it holds. A tenfold statement worked best for our family because it allowed us to include the ideas presented by our kids.

And now, I present to you our family mission statement.

The Battles Family Mission Statement

1. We love God first and foremost. We are a Christ-centered family. Our primary goal is to worship God, obey His commands, and have a personal relationship with Christ.

2. We strive to love one another as we love ourselves. This is our golden rule: to treat others as we also want to be treated.

3. We work hard, individually and as a team.

4. We respect one another by sharing, practicing good manners, listening, and speaking with kind words and tone of voice.

5. We continue to learn together always and teach one another new skills.

6. We serve those in need. We seek to help the less fortunate.

7. We strive to live a life of integrity and purity. We do this by keeping our minds, bodies, and hearts pure.

8. We practice fiscal responsibility, which includes tithing, saving, and giving.

9. We play together, have fun, enjoy life, and go on adventures as a family.

10. We seek to fulfill God's purpose for each of our lives through finding and doing His will.

Because our Christian faith is our top family value, we selected a verse from the Bible that aligned with each of the above statements. If your faith is a top value, you, too, may want to look up Scripture verses that align with the components of your family mission statement and record them as a means of making your statement even more meaningful. You can use a Bible concordance or a website, such as BibleGateway.com, that allows you to search for specific terms.

WHAT TO DO WITH YOUR MISSION STATEMENT

Once you have established your family mission statement, you have a basis for your family's hierarchy of importance—a clear expression of what your family most values and considers important. Print the mission statement, frame it, and display it in a highly visible place in your home. Doing so provides a daily reminder to your family members of their purpose and values, as well as the contributions they made, individually, to the statement.

In our home, I went a step further, for the sake of aesthetics, and hired someone to pen our statement in calligraphy. I then framed it for displaying on the desk in our kitchen, where we daily see this reminder of our mission statement. We are a team, our family, together for a reason. Therefore, the decisions we make, and especially the way we choose to spend our time, is filtered through this mission statement we developed together.

Your family mission statement should become the lens through which you decide what is important and worthy of your time—and what is not. Knowing what is most significant and of the highest value to your family is the first step toward creating a life in which you are easily able to recognize how you should be spending your time. Your family mission statement keeps you focused on your family's priorities.

HOBBIES AND SELF-CARE ARE PRIORITIES, TOO

Once you have determined your personal hierarchy of importance and your family's purpose, as defined by your mission statement, you will be ready for the next step: assessing your hobbies. Hobbies are an important and valuable part of life, as long as they are not permitted to monopolize your time and energy.

My hobbies and interests have changed over time, and it's likely that yours will do the same. What were once meaningful pastimes for me— downhill skiing, baking, singing in the choir—are now less important. I had to choose to let go of certain activities, entirely or at least a little bit, in order to make more time for my family. Having children is a sure way to shift your hobbies and interests. When my husband and I became parents, our lives stopped being just ours; we had little people counting on us—little people who needed a lot of our time. Now, just because I've released some hobbies for now, while my kids are young, doesn't mean I can't pick up those hobbies again in the future. Kids are little for just a short while. Their early childhood is a season of great importance. God has placed my kids' development—spiritual, mental, physical, and emotional—in my hands. Skiing three days a week, as I did in college, doesn't seem that important when I really consider my responsibility toward my children.

Some hobbies are appreciated to different degrees at different stages of our lives. For example, several years ago, my husband and I took our children skiing and had a great time, but it was far different from my memories of skiing with groups of friends in my twenties. I don't mind taking a break from some hobbies and activities because I have a greater purpose that God has called me to in this season of life.

In suggesting that you consider taking a break from or letting go of certain hobbies, I am not advocating an all-work-and-no-play approach. Far from it! Whether you are single or married, a parent or not, everyone needs to take breaks and have fun. Keeping up with hobbies and activities that we enjoy can offer a change from our day-to-day routine that is essential to our own mental, emotional, and physical health. Don't just get rid of your hobbies if you think they don't align with your family mission statement. Personal goals are important, and hobbies and pastimes you enjoy should be part of those personal goals. You may not have the same amount of time for these interests as you did before you were a parent, but that doesn't mean you should eliminate all of them. Maintain those interests that rank highest for you, especially if they offer a weekly break. One summer before becoming a mom, I started skydiving (I do have a daredevil streak of weirdness in me); but now, with little kids who depend on me, I decided to give up that hobby. Now, I participate in the book club I started, I'm an avid reader, and I blog and write. These are activities I enjoy that keep my sense of who I am alive and thriving. We don't give up everything we love just because we now have children to raise. There needs to be a balance to this parenting thing.

Find at least a few hours a week that you can carve out to spend on a personal hobby or interest. By "carve out," I mean actually put it on your calendar so it won't be mere wishful thinking. Make a pointed effort to schedule your personal activity or break on a weekly basis. Every parent should engage in this vital form of self-care. If weeks go by without your taking time out for yourself, you'll risk succumbing to burnout. Burned-out parents are likelier to lash out at their kids and to exhibit resentfulness, moodiness, and hostility. If you feel yourself tending toward these kinds of attitudes and behaviors, you should examine your life honestly. Are you engaging weekly in activities that refresh you? I realize that participating in favorite pastimes can prove very difficult if you have young children in the home. You may be the sole caregiver for an infant or toddler, but that doesn't have to keep you from finding an outlet for yourself, a way to engage in self-care.

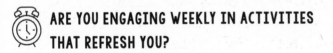

ARE YOU ENGAGING WEEKLY IN ACTIVITIES THAT REFRESH YOU?

When my husband and I were foster parents to a baby girl, the only real downtime I had was when she was napping; however, I myself often napped at the same time because I was fatigued from being pregnant. It wasn't long before I found a group of girlfriends to walk with. Three days a week, we would meet near their kids' school and walk and talk together for about an hour. I always looked forward to these walks. The baby would sleep in the stroller, taking her morning nap, while I got in some brisk exercise and gained some new friends through deep conversations. This was a season when I couldn't go anywhere without the baby. Despite my deep love for and attachment to our foster baby, I knew that I needed to prioritize self-care. Three hours a week of exercise and conversation with some girlfriends was a great solution for that season of my life. Today, finding myself in a completely different season of life, I have changed my sources of self-care to writing, blogging, reading, and spending time with friends.

Self-care is crucial for every parent—moms and dads alike. My husband and I both recognize this fact, and so, if he wants to go watch a game with a friend, I encourage it. He needs that break, just as I need breaks throughout the week. We all need downtime so that we can come back to our families feeling refreshed and reenergized.

EMPOWERED TO SAY NO

You have created a family mission statement, you've determined your personal hierarchy of importance, and you've probably figured out a hobby or two that you can turn to for a few hours of self-care each week. Now it's time to take action and use your family mission statement to evaluate the activities you're involved in and begin saying no to any activities that don't fit. If an activity does not bring joy to you or your family, and if it does not support the values articulated in your family mission statement, then you should try saying no.

I was once asked by a friend of mine to join a women's soccer league with her. As much as I wanted to spend time with my friend, and as greatly as I appreciate a good workout, I immediately recognized that this activity did not align with the values expressed in my family's mission statement, and neither did it fit within my hierarchy of importance. Furthermore, I knew that soccer is not a sport that makes me feel relaxed or refreshed. Attending practices and playing in games would feel to me more like work than self-care. So, I politely declined my friend's request, following up my answer by scheduling a visit with her over coffee.

Learning to say no is not easy, especially because an invitation to do something with a friend or a loved one often comes across as a compliment we don't want to turn down. Learn to say no, but find a way to maintain connections and friendships in spite of your no. You may not be able to serve on your child's school's Parent Teacher Organization (PTO) with your friend because the meetings conflict with your Bible study schedule. Instead of turning that no into a friendship-defeating conversation, you might consider inviting that friend and her family for dinner. A onetime commitment for a dinner date is a win over a drawn-out commitment to monthly PTO meetings when you are trying to find ways to cut activities from your schedule rather than adding them.

Again, learning to say no is a process—but it's an empowering one to master. If something does not align with your mission statement, doesn't add value to your hierarchy of importance, and won't bring you joy, then you should say no. Don't ever commit to something out of a fear of disappointing someone. Your real priority is your family and the values you have articulated in your mission statement.

 DON'T EVER COMMIT TO SOMETHING OUT OF A FEAR OF DISAPPOINTING SOMEONE.

I almost always say yes when it comes to volunteering in my kids' activities. I have recently served as a cheer coach, preschool music teacher, and Good News Club music leader. All these are activities that allow me to participate while spending time with my kids. In addition, they are activities I enjoy, they align with our family mission statement, and they create opportunities for me to spend valuable time with my kids.

You will find more fulfillment from activities that align with your values, support your purpose, and bring you joy. It becomes easier to say no to activities when you know your purpose and your values. Your mission statement gives you permission to say no to things that don't align with your purpose. Give yourself permission to say no, and get rid of any activities that don't serve an intentional purpose in your life and don't give you joy.

CHAPTER 2:

DON'T DO TOO MUCH FOR YOUR KIDS

Some parents find themselves burned out and exhausted from doing activities they have no business doing—tasks and chores that ought to belong to their kids. Doing too much for our kids is often our own fault because of one or more of the following three problems: (1) we have them overscheduled, participating in far too many activities; (2) we helicopter parent, trying to live our kids' lives for them; and (3) we fail to delegate enough household duties to them.

It is time to assess these three areas of your life. There is no time better than the present to start making changes if you find that you are doing too much for your kids.

OVERSCHEDULED KIDS

Most kids these days participate in multiple activities during the week. Some kids are overscheduled, with a different activity and a different place to be every day after school. When children are overscheduled in such a manner, parents become more chauffeurs than parents. The prime time of the day for connecting with our kids—after school—is instead filled with coaches, music instructors, club leaders, and so forth. While these individuals may be worthy people, they are essentially taking away your key parenting time, potentially eroding the soil of your children's souls into which you are trying to seed and plant your morals, values, and beliefs.

The only way to instill your family's values into the hearts and minds of your children is by spending time with your kids—quality time, in quantity. Am I suggesting you stop all activities? Certainly not. My own kids are involved in activities several days of the week. The goal is to assess our kids' activities and see how closely they align with our families' mission statements. Are we keeping our kids busy for the sake of our being involved in their lives? Or are we letting them choose activities to participate in based on their personal passions and the potential life lessons to be learned that align with our values?

When kids are overscheduled, the parents can't help but become overscheduled, as well. Parents are usually the ones responsible for shuttling their kids to and from activities and sport practices all week long, and even the weekends tend to become centered on game times, music recitals, performance schedules, birthday parties, and the like. Our families' freedom and quality time together declines sharply when our kids are involved in too many activities. Weekends cease to be our own, and our kids' activities end up dictating our existence because their involvement in these activities depends on our driving them to and from events day after day. Meals on the go, often eaten in the car, become a regular habit because nobody is ever home to sit at the dinner table together to eat.

 WHEN KIDS ARE OVERSCHEDULED, THE PARENTS CAN'T HELP BUT BECOME OVERSCHEDULED, AS WELL.

Overscheduling robs our kids of energy and places impossible demands on our schedules as parents. Let's take back at least some of our time by reducing and eliminating activities that are not essential to your family or children.

SIGNS THAT A CHILD MAY BE OVERSCHEDULED

Extracurricular activities need to be balanced. Overscheduling kids isn't healthy; it taxes them emotionally, physically, and mentally. There are specific behaviors that act as warning signs to let you know you have a child who is overscheduled. Not sure whether one or more of your children is overscheduled? Try answering the following questions. The more times you answer yes, the likelier it is that your child could stand to have a reduction in activities.

1. Does your child often act crabby and irritable?

2. Are your child's grades declining?

3. Does your child seem anxious?

4. Does your child constantly seek approval from the adults in his or her life?

5. Does your child complain about his or her extracurricular activities and express an unwillingness to continue participating?

6. Does your child have temper tantrums or exhibit resistance when it comes time to head out the door for a scheduled activity?

7. Does your child complain of physical aches and pains when it comes time to head out the door for a scheduled activity?

8. Does your child have difficulty keeping track of what activity he or she is to participate in on a given day?

9. Does your child seem to "zone out" in front of any variety of electronic devices (television, tablet, iPad, etc.)?

10. Is your child's schedule draining your own energy level?

11. Can you recall the last time your child had the option of doing nothing at all?

12. If your child were to find himself or herself without any scheduled activities, how would he or she act? Would it be possible for your child to entertain himself or herself, or would he or she seek direction from you or another adult?

13. Does your child complain that he or she finds no joy in an extracurricular activity?

14. Does your child seem disconnected from his or her friends?

If you answered yes to more than just a few of the above questions, you should sit down and assess, with input from your child, his or her activities and involvements. The solution is simple: Do less. Start

DON'T DO TOO MUCH FOR YOUR KIDS 31

by eliminating just one activity per week. If that step doesn't seem to make a difference, then you can eliminate another activity. Begin by eliminating the activities your child is the least passionate about. You may desperately want your child to learn to play the piano or another instrument, but if your child dreads practicing and gets anxiety over attending music lessons, maybe it's time to let it go—at least for now. Our dreams for our kids aren't always their dreams for themselves. It's fine to let your children try many different extracurricular activities in order to discover their passions; just remember, they can't do them all. If they identify something that they truly do not enjoy, and they begin to develop anxiety about that activity, then it is almost certain that the activity should stop. Just be careful how and when you withdraw your child from an activity, because you want to instill in your kids the importance of being committed and seeing things through. Pulling them out of soccer mid-season is not the best way to emphasize commitment. In this case, it may be best to simply let your child finish the season without signing up him or her for the team the following year. A lot depends on your child's behavior and on the degree to which he or she is overscheduled.

When she was very young, my daughter loved dressing up in costumes and dancing around the house. She wanted to start dance classes, so I enrolled her in a weekly class that combined ballet and tap dance. It started in the fall, and for the first few weeks, she seemed to enjoy herself. By the middle of the school year, however, I could tell that she no longer enjoyed this activity. Whatever the reason—a lack of fondness for the dance instructor, a failure to bond with the other girls in the class, or indifference toward learning a particular dance technique—she was clearly anxious about dance. She was in a foul mood on dance days and began throwing temper tantrums every week when it was time to leave for class.

My first instinct was to follow through and have her finish the year, but I quickly realized that this activity was not worth the anxiety it was causing my daughter, especially given how young she was. I also perceived that the structure of the dance classes did not jive with her creativity level at that particular stage of her development—a time when she preferred, above anything else, being home with her brothers, as they were building forts out of bedsheets and chairs or playing "school" with stuffed animals for students. Creative play was her strong point, and this strength was not being encouraged by her dance classes. We withdrew her from dance just before the scheduled recital. This was not an easy decision, especially since we had already paid over $100 for her recital costume. However, it was the best decision in the long run. Hindsight is always 20/20, but in these situations, you just have to make the best decision with the information you have and the behaviors you see. No decision will ever be perfect. If I had known then what I know now, I would have taken her out of dance sooner.

I am so glad we withdrew her from dance when we did. She took a year off and then asked to start classes again. I found a different dance studio that encouraged more creativity and self-expression through dance. It was a much better match for my daughter, who now loves dance.

Backing out of an activity can happen for a time; it does not need to be forever. Sometimes your child just needs a break—or maybe *you* do. Life is made of seasons. If your child is in a season of seeming to dread a certain activity, then you should seriously think about having him or her stop that activity for now. You can always pick it up again later.

Children develop differently from one another and need time and space to mature and grow. An overabundance of activities diminishes their creative development through too much adult structured time, so make sure you give them time to be themselves. Let them be kids! Running around outside and playing with other kids, riding their bikes around the neighborhood with no particular plan or destination, climbing trees simply for the sake of adventure…kids need free time to just be kids; time to explore, create, dream, and imagine. Imagination plays a huge role in their development and largely predicts their eventual success as adults. The World Economic Forum (2017)[1] predicted that creativity would be the second-most sought-after skill in the workplace by the year 2020. Yet, their data also shows that creativity has diminished drastically among children since 1990. Don't underestimate the benefits of free time. Your children need the freedom for imaginative play. And don't underestimate the potential benefits of boredom, for a state of being bored is often what is required for your children to tap into their creativity.

 KIDS NEED FREE TIME TO JUST BE KIDS.

Free time doesn't happen if your kids are so overscheduled that when they get home from school or an extracurricular activity, they just want to zone out in front of their electronic devices or go to bed. If they are physically and mentally exhausted at the end of a day filled with school and followed up with extracurricular activities, there is no room for imaginative play. They need time outside of activities, when the daylight remains and they still have energy left in their bodies. This allows them the space and freedom to imagine, create, and play. If they have activities every day after school that zap their energy, and then have homework to complete, and then head straight to bed, they are not getting the free time they need for healthy development.

Don't rob your children of the joys of childhood by overschedul-ing them. And don't allow overscheduling to turn you into more of a

---

1. World Economic Forum, "This is the one skill your child needs for the jobs of the future," 15 September 2017, https://www.weforum.org/agenda/2017/09/skills-children-need-work-future-play-lego/.

chauffeur than a parent. Giving your children the time to just be kids gives you time to be the parent. At home, after school, time spent together as a family just *being* is one of the best gifts there is. Take some time to evaluate your kids' schedules and see where you can free up some time to just *be*.

THE PITFALLS OF HELICOPTER PARENTING

You've probably heard of "helicopter parenting," a term coined by child-development researchers Foster Cline and Jim Fay in 1990 to identify parents who hover protectively around their children, never giving them a chance to work things out on their own and learn to manage risks.[2] Helicopter parenting is a style of raising kids that can severely deplete your time and energy. If you want to reclaim more time for yourself and maintain a higher level of energy, consider whether you might be "helicopter parenting" your kids; if so, make an effort to back off. Helicopter parents are people who care a lot about their kids, but often they care so much that they end up doing too much for their kids.

Why are so many moms and dads today falling into a pattern of helicopter parenting? One reason is a culture of competition that has parents working harder and doing more to "help" their kids, only to result in kids who can't do anything for themselves. It is one thing to help a child with her homework when she is struggling and asking for help, and a far different thing to hover over a child every night, strictly supervising the completion of every project (and maybe stepping in to improve the work when a lack is perceived).

Helicopter parenting takes attentive parenting to the extreme, so that it ceases to be beneficial and instead harms the children's chances

2. Sonja Haller, "What type of parent are you? Lawnmower? Helicopter? Attachment? Tiger? Free-range?" *USA Today*, 19 September 2018, https://www.usatoday.com/story/life/allthemoms/2018/09/19/parenting-terms-explained-lawnmower-helicopter-attachment-tiger-free-range-dolphin-elephant/1357612002/.

of surviving on their own once they leave home to begin life as adults. Overparenting harms our kids in the long run. Helicopter parenting doesn't promote the ultimate well-being of our kids, and it imposes a huge burden on our time and energy. If we fail to let go and refuse to allow our kids to tackle their assignments, projects, and activities on their own, we are doing them a disservice in the long run. They need to learn to problem-solve for themselves, or with minimal guidance. Parents should not do for their children what the children should be doing for themselves.

 LEAD BY EXAMPLE AS YOU CHALLENGE YOUR CHILDREN TO PICK THEMSELVES UP, BRUSH THEMSELVES OFF, AND TRY AGAIN.

When we helicopter parent, we use up time that would be better spent elsewhere. You learned arithmetic and algebra long ago—why would you do your kids' math homework for them? It's their turn to learn. Stop doing things that they can do or that they need to learn to do for themselves. Again, it's about minimal guidance. Provide just enough guidance to support their efforts to tackle the work themselves, and no more than that. You are doing your kids a favor when you back off from overparenting, because you're helping them mature and develop—a process that must include room for failure. Life lessons are rarely learned by success alone. In most cases, it's the mistakes we make that propel our greatest learning experiences. Failure is where grit and determination are honed. Lead by example as you challenge your children to pick themselves up, brush themselves off, and try again. Don't grab the reins and do the work for them just because they failed the first time. Rather, point them in the right direction and tell them to try again.

When my daughter was learning to ride a bike, she wanted me to hold on to the back of the seat the entire time. She didn't want me to let go because she feared falling. We stopped and talked about it, and I explained that falling is part of learning to ride a bike. I told her that she would probably fall—multiple times, even—and would need to get back up each time, pedal hard to get the bike going, and try to go as far as she could without (or before) falling again.

Just as falling is part of learning to ride a bike, failing is part of finding success. Nobody masters the piano and plays like Mozart after just one lesson. Instead, we start small and build on our skills. From our mistakes, we learn how to correct our errors. If we don't allow our kids to experience small failures as they grow up, then when they experience big failures in young adulthood, they won't have any idea how to pick themselves back up and persist. If we don't allow our children to experience small-scale failures early in life, then how can we expect them to weather major disappointments later in life? If we are constantly protecting our kids from their failures by doing things for them, then they won't develop those skills that they will need to be successful adults, and even the smallest of letdowns later in life is sure to break them. We must give them the space to make mistakes so that they can develop perseverance and learn how to handle disappointments and failures.

SIX TIPS TO PREVENT HELICOPTER PARENTING

Here are six tips to help you avoid any tendencies toward helicopter parenting.

1. **Let them do it themselves.** If they can do something for themselves, go ahead and let them. Even though you could probably do it faster and better, they won't learn if you keep doing it for them. If they are capable of making their own bed, then have them do it on a daily basis. If they can get themselves dressed, then let them do it for themselves. If they can pour their own

cereal and milk for breakfast, then let them do it. Don't do it for them. This tip is probably the most important when it comes to correcting any helicopter parenting. By letting kids do what they can do for themselves, you're teaching them to be responsible, capable, self-reliant human beings.

2. **Resist the urge to fix things for them.** If you see that your son's school project could be improved if you added a few more sentences, restrain yourself and let it be. It's his project, not yours. Allow your kids' work to be wholly their own. If they make their beds and the results aren't "perfect," let it be. You can talk to them about working on improving their techniques or approaches if you deem it necessary, but you need to let them do the work themselves. Additionally, if you keep improving on their work, whether it's their best work or not, you may be unconsciously communicating to them that their work is not worthwhile or good enough.

3. **Don't project your emotions onto your kids.** Maybe your child is going through something that, were you in her shoes, would cause you extreme anxiety or worry. Even if that is the case, don't assume how she's feeling and project your own emotions onto her. Let's say your daughter has a piano recital coming up, and you feel nervous for her. Don't compound her own worries by continually asking her if she's feeling nervous or fearful. Instead, speak positively, offering reassurance, encouragement, and support. She doesn't need you piling your emotions on top of hers. Your children can sense your emotions even when you haven't verbalized them. They sense when you are worried, anxious, concerned, or doubting. Don't feel the need to explain how you're feeling if your emotions might prove burdensome to them.

4. **Give your children the chance to fail.** We all learn from our failures. How can we expect our kids to learn how to overcome failure if we never let them fail in the first place? Allowing them to experience failure gives them the opportunity to build perseverance and grit. If you are constantly trying to prevent any and all failure, you are expending time and energy that is not benefitting your children in the long run. The next time your son forgets his lunch at home, let him deal with the consequences. He may have to figure out how to get credit for a school cafeteria lunch that day or ask some friends to share some of their food. Let it be a learning experience. I assure you he'll be a lot less likely to forget his lunch going forward!

5. **Recognize your own discomfort and push through it.** It can be very uncomfortable standing by and watching our children fall and fail, especially if we are accustomed to routinely rescuing them from failure. Recognize your feelings, process them, and keep moving forward while standing your ground. Don't cave under the pressure of your emotions. Keep reminding yourself that you are doing this for the sake of your children's character and for helping them develop important skills.

6. **Don't make your children the center of your world.** If your life revolves around your children, you are bound to take their successes and their failures personally. Your sense of your self-worth should not be based on your children's behaviors and performances. If it is, then their successes and failures become your primary focus. You won't be able to let them fail if you perceive their failures as your own failures, especially preventable failures. You will end up with grown-up children who don't know how to function in the world. Your constant hand-holding and helping them do everything will prevent them from ever becoming independent and capable individuals.

THE BENEFITS OF REFRAINING FROM HELICOPTER PARENTING

When you release yourself from the bondage of helicopter parenting, you gain for yourself greater freedom and a more open schedule. All the time and effort you had been pouring into the micromanagement of your child's life can now be channeled elsewhere in your own life. Remember those hobbies you haven't had time for in a while? Well, you now have the time. You no longer need to hover over your kids and provide continual correction while they do their homework each night. You can do your own thing nearby, making yourself available if they should need any help, and your kids will be blessed to see you enjoying a worthwhile hobby. Perhaps you want to get back into (or into for the first time) drawing, writing, or painting. Make homework time an opportunity to pursue your own hobby alongside your children while they do their school projects. You are released from the hovering of helicopter parenting and the bondage it brings, and yet you are still available to your kids to assist and answer questions as needed. Your kids will still need you from time to time, so be there in the same room, available to answer their questions. However, you no longer need to do their homework. Their homework is theirs. No more hovering allowed.

THE BENEFITS TO CHILDREN

Parenting is a marathon, not a sprint, and it is important to retain this perspective as you consider the entire journey. Pushing our kids toward overachievement at a young age is likely to burn them out—not to mention ourselves. What a shame for the children who peak at ten years of age because they had helicopter parents micromanaging their lives.

I started training my children to exercise personal responsibility when they were very young. By age five, my twins, who were enrolled at a full-time preschool that was serious about academics yet also emphasized creative play, were given homework assignments several days a week. It didn't require many reminders from me for them to learn the responsibility of getting their homework folders from their backpack each day after school. Once I stopped reminding them, there were certain days when they would forget about their homework or miss an assignment. I was okay with this, because the resulting feeling of failure would only reinforce their desire to be more responsible in the future, and it would prevent them from being devastated by minor setbacks later in life. Completing their homework is my kids' duty, not mine. I may need to read the directions aloud to them and explain what they are to do, but they are responsible for getting it done. I don't continually remind them to do it; I don't hover over them while they work and make sure they're doing it correctly. They may make mistakes, but that is part of the learning process. They don't need me to push them to be perfect or overachievers. In time, given the proper space and opportunities, they will shine on their own, based on their own merit and achievements. And when that happens, I will be proud of my children because I know they did it themselves, striving to fulfill a personal goal rather than merely appeasing their pushy mother. They will be successful in any pursuit when their heart is in it and they claim ownership of what they are trying to accomplish. My job as a parent is to support and encourage them along the way.

Your children will learn grit if you allow them to fail and give them the chance to succeed without your pushing them from behind the entire journey. Children who are overparented don't develop grit. They won't learn how to pick themselves up after failure, because their helicopter parents are there to pick them up before they even start falling. Allowing your children to experience failure will help them develop the skills and tenacity they need to persevere and ultimately become successful as adults. Let them run the marathon on their own merit. Run beside them and encourage them the entire journey, but don't hoist them onto your back and run the race for them.

DELEGATING IS KEY

I have traveled to Guatemala on numerous humanitarian trips over the years. During my first visit, I was astonished and shocked to see young children on the streets working to help earn an income for their family. I once paid to have a little girl who was ten years old braid my hair. She sold me some beautiful handwoven material that she then wove into the braids she made in my hair. The girl told me that she had gone to school for several years but stopped because her family needed her help earning money. This experience left quite an impression on me. This little girl was able to work the crowds in a touristy area of Guatemala to sell her wares and market her skills to earn money so her family could survive. On subsequent trips to Guatemala, I purchased packages of gum and candy, and some souvenir trinkets, from kids on the streets as young as five years of age, all of whom smiled as they sold their wares and counted their earnings. On one occasion, I even helped one little girl count the money I had paid her. Looking back, I often think about how capable and hardworking these kids were. They could barely count money and make change, yet they were selling goods on the street to support their families. If small children in Guatemala can do that, then my kids can certainly make their own beds, wash the dishes, sweep the floors, and more.

Our kids are far more competent and capable than we give them credit for being. They may not do their jobs with the same skill or competence that we would, but how will they ever learn these skills and improve upon them if we don't let them try? I am a strong believer in assigning kids specific chores and responsibilities.

 OUR KIDS ARE FAR MORE COMPETENT AND CAPABLE THAN WE GIVE THEM CREDIT FOR BEING.

Kids of all ages need daily responsibilities. These responsibilities are not only for their own good but also for the good of the entire family. It is likely that the idea of working together as a team is now, or will become, part of your family mission statement. What better way to work together as a team than to work together to keep the house clean and tidy? Not only will chores teach your kids important skills for later in life, they will give your children an opportunity to take pride in their work when they see how the fruits of their chores have helped the family.

Too many parents are performing almost all the household work. Again, kids are more than capable of doing a fair share of the work! Be enthusiastic about household chores, and your kids will feed off your enthusiasm. Let them know that they are mature enough to start helping, whatever the chore may be. Make them a part of the household team as early as possible. Kids as young as eighteen months can begin helping around the house. Build on your children's capabilities, adding chores as they age.

By delegating household chores, you are not only empowering your kids; you are giving yourself more freedom and time. You may not see results instantly. There is always a learning curve when it comes to chores. It may take a week or two, or more, for your kids to get the hang of things. Just be patient and persistent. Eventually, with your encouraging guidance, your children will start taking ownership of their assigned chores. They may even seek additional responsibilities, or start to identify particular jobs they truly enjoy.

The effort and time required for teaching your children specific household jobs are well worth it, because their capability to complete a multitude of chores is a gift to the family and to them. Not only does it alleviate some of your workload as a parent, but it paves the way for your children to become capable, responsible people who will be well prepared to teach chores to their own children one day.

CHAPTER 3:

KEEP AN ORGANIZED HOME AND AN ORGANIZED LIFE

Benjamin Franklin observed, "For every minute spent in organizing, an hour is earned." This quote resonates with me to the very core of my being. I have found an organized home and an organized life crucial to my thriving and success.

Keeping an organized home is a key to effective time management. I have lived long enough to know that when I condition myself to put the car keys back in exactly the same place when I get home each day, then I will be able to easily locate those keys when I need them the next morning. The same is true about every item I need throughout any given day. If I can easily find it because it has a "home" within the home and has been put in that home after every use, then my life becomes easier and more streamlined. Searching for an item you need can be a huge waste of time and energy.

If you tend to waste time searching for keys or other household items on a regular basis, this chapter is for you. Keeping an organized home is not about making more work for yourself. True, it takes some extra effort to get organized in the first place, but when you put a system in place that you are committed to maintaining, your household starts running like a well-oiled machine. Be sure to get your family involved in the organization process, so that they are likelier to stick to the plan. Establish a rule that if you use something, you put it back where you found it. This brings me to my first tip on having an organized home:

TIP #1: EVERYTHING HAS A HOME

Everything you own should have a home. What does this mean, exactly? It means that if you buy something from the hardware store, the market, online, or elsewhere, you already know where that item will be stored. Every item in your household belongs in a specific location within your home. This location—where each item belongs—is its "home."

I don't care whether an item brings you joy, or whether you think you might need it a year or two from now. All that truly matters is your ability to answer this question: "Does the item have a home, and do I know where that home is?" If you have so much stuff that you couldn't possibly find a home for every item, it is time to pare down and declutter. Get rid of anything you haven't used in years and have no definite plans for using in the future. If you are like me and you don't know whether you are ever going to use the mini salt and pepper shakers you purchased for each person's place setting for a special dinner party, but you certainly hope to use them, don't give them away; just make sure they have a home, so that you can easily find them when the day of that long-anticipated dinner party finally arrives. If your house is so cluttered and disorganized that it would take you hours to find those sets of mini salt and pepper shakers, then you either need to reorganize or get rid of some things. I prefer the former, because organizing allows me to keep more things!

 WHEN ORGANIZING, ASK YOURSELF THIS QUESTION: "DOES THE ITEM HAVE A HOME, AND DO I KNOW WHERE THAT HOME IS?"

Benjamin Franklin also published the book that popularized the phrase "A penny saved is a penny earned." I don't believe in wasting things, but wasting time searching for things can be just as fruitless. Therefore, if you want to keep, say, birthday gift bags for later reuse, then you should designate a specific drawer, cabinet, or box for those bags. They shouldn't be scattered among assorted drawers, stuffed beneath beds, or crammed inside random cabinets. If the gift bags have a specific home, then the next time your daughter needs to wrap a present for a friend's birthday party, you will have saved yourself from having to run to the store and spend more money; you will also have avoided having to spend time searching the house for a usable gift bag. When you have decided that you are going to save reusable gift bags, and you have designated a specific location as their home, you will be able to sort through the entire stack at one time and select a suitable bag within one minute, thereby saving yourself time and money.

THE BIN METHOD

The "bin method" is a method of organization I've been using ever since I coined the phrase over twenty years ago. Even when I was young and single, I used bins for storing my belongings because it helped me stay organized and also made it easier to move into and out of college dorms, then back home again, then to my first apartment, then to my first house, and so on. The bin method is for everyone! It just works. It is not expensive, either. I started my bin method with shoebox bins from The Dollar Tree. Most dollar discount stores sell shoebox-size bins at an affordable price. This means getting twenty of them in your home is worth every penny spent. The ability to find the right voltage of batteries, right when you need them, is like money in the bank. On the other hand, having to go out and buy a new package of batteries because you can't find the last pack you purchased is a waste of money. The bin method allows you to use what you have. You can more easily use what you have when you know what you have, because you know exactly where to look.

The bin method makes having a "home" for all the smaller stuff in your home feasible. I like to use the bin method in the kitchen pantry, the bathroom linen closet, the garage shelves, the playroom closet, the upper shelves of our laundry room, our bedroom closets, and under certain beds. The best place to start putting the bin method to use in your home is probably the kitchen or the laundry room. Select an upper shelf or cabinet that offers a wide, open space. (You may have to look past any clutter or junk currently being stored there.) Those speakers from 1999 can probably go to Goodwill or another charity, if they will accept them. Once you have identified some prime real estate in your upper closet or pantry shelving and eliminated any junk formerly housed there, it's time to get to work.

Measure the space you want to utilize, then shop for bins that best fit the space. In my personal experience, shoebox-size bins are the most versatile, since they work well inside cabinets and on shelves. They also stack nicely, to a height of four or five.

In our kitchen pantry, I use the bin method to store kitchen supplies and houseware items that we don't use on a daily basis but will likely need at some point in the future—for example, seasonal cookie cutters. Keeping them in the same place—a tad inconvenient to access, but a familiar space nonetheless—allows me to make use of them year after year instead of having to go out and purchase new ones every time my kids want to bake Christmas cookies.

Whenever you purchase something, especially if it's small in size or rarely used, make sure you give it a home in a bin. That way, all those miscellaneous items that usually end up lost and scattered in various drawers and cabinets will now have a home that is clearly labeled. This makes finding things in the future a breeze.

If my husband is searching for skewers for the barbecue, I can simply tell him to check the proper bin in the pantry marked "skewers." If, by some chance, that bin is empty, he'll know we need to buy some more. Nine times out of ten, when he's looking for a household item that we have used in the past, he will find it in its pantry bin. This method saves us from purchasing items that we already own, because we are able to find them easily when we want them. Many people often end up buying a replacement for items they can't locate quickly enough in their homes. Save yourself both money and time by employing the bin method!

Using the upper shelves of a closet or pantry for lesser-used items is wise because it lets you take advantage of all available storage space. Go ahead and stack the bins as high as you safely can; if they contain items you rarely use, it should not be a major inconvenience to take the extra time to climb up and reach them on the occasion when you need those items. I can't reach the top bin of the stack in my pantry, which is why I keep a small folding step stool in the pantry, too. (This means the pantry is the home for my step stool, and I never have trouble finding it when I need it.)

Besides the pantry, another great area to tackle with the bin method is your junk drawer—you know, the place where you've been stashing a mix of just about everything, including batteries, screwdrivers, small canisters of bug spray, coupons, office supplies, and so on. Empty the drawer(s) and separate the contents into categories: flashlights in one pile, batteries in another pile, tools in another pile, et cetera. Once you have sorted the drawer contents into piles, you can transfer like items into bins, label the bins accordingly, and stack those bins in their new home.

If your kids are old enough, have them help out with the sorting and organizing. That way, they'll know where to find the things they need (and also where to store those things when they are finished with them). It also teaches them a useful method for staying organized. When they ask for masking tape for a school project, you can point them to the appropriate bin, and before long they won't be asking for help finding anything (well, just about anything).

For the first several months after sorting things into bins, I usually had to give my kids (and my husband) the gentle reminder to put things back when they were finished with them. The good news is, organizational behaviors can be learned by any person, regardless of age or background. Pretty soon, your spouse and kids will be locating what they need and returning it to its rightful spot without any help from you.

It's all about creating new habits. When you start using the bin method, make it a point to put things back in their bins immediately after using them. This discipline creates a habit of putting things back in their home. Otherwise, the items end up sitting on a counter for a few days and then getting shoved into a drawer or stuffed in a cabinet when the doorbell rings and you have unexpected guests. Don't be a "drawer-stuffer"! Break old habits by starting new ones.

BIN METHOD LABELS

When I first blogged about the bin method, countless readers wanted to know what my bin labels said. I was happy to offer some examples, though I cautioned them that everyone's bins should have unique labels reflecting the unique assortment of items they are storing. Below are the labels from a few of the regularly accessed bins I have kept over the years.

- Chalk

- Babyproofing/childproofing items

- Electrical outlet plug covers

- Skewers

- Extra silverware (for dinner parties)

- Matches and lighters

- Cookie cutters

- Plastic gloves

- Cake decorating supplies

- Scotch tape and floral tape

- Duct tape and masking tape

- Luggage locks and padlocks

- Batteries

- First-aid items (Band-Aids, Neosporin, gauze, ACE Bandages, etc.)

- Shoe polish and extra shoelaces

- Wood repair kit

- 3M hooks and 3M double-sided tape

- Tealights and candles

- Fuses

- Flashlights

- Sewing kits

- Zip ties

- Twine and thin rope

- Extra pens and pencils

- Sunscreen and bug spray

- Photos

- Clamps

- Extra kitchen sponges

- Note cards and thank-you notes

- Birthday cards

Use labels on the outsides of your bins. Any basic adhesive label that you can write on legibly will work. I prefer medium-sized white labels, so that I can easily read the list of contents without having to look up close.

Returning to that junk drawer: I have a kitchen drawer where I keep basic items and office supplies we use on an almost daily basis, such as pens, sticky pads, scissors, paperclips, a stapler, and stamps. I organize these items with a compartmentalized caddy designed for wide, shallow drawers. Each item has its own little home within the drawer. Even so, this drawer tends to get messy every few months, and I have tasked my kids with taking everything out and putting it back again neatly when they have made a mess of the contents. It's amazing how quickly they have learned to put things back in the correct compartments after three or four times of having to clean up the drawer.

The bathroom cabinet is another location where I keep a tall stack of bins, some of which house extra toiletry items that I tend to buy in bulk, such as toothbrushes and toothpaste, soap, razors, lotion, candles, vitamins, and first-aid supplies. I also have bins that are slightly larger and more accessible for storing medicine, nail care supplies (bottles of polish, bottles of polish remover, nail files, clippers, and so on), and hair care supplies (curlers, hair dryers, hair brushes that may not be used every day, et cetera.).

The goal of the bin method is not to have everything perfect in your home. My home is not perfect, I can assure you! No, the idea behind the bin method is having a designated home for every item so that you can easily find things exactly when you need them. If you are rushing out the door to help decorate at your kids' school, and you offered to bring the tape, you can save yourself the embarrassment of arriving late because of having to turn your house upside down—and you can save the expense of having to stop at the store—if you know exactly where you store your extra tape. It would also be frustrating to have to make a stop on the way to school if you were already in a rush, and even more so after running around searching your house for something you know you have sitting around the house somewhere.

Giving your things a home is about creating a space for everything so you can easily find what you need when you need it. Clearly labeling the bins saves time, too. Never haphazardly toss things into bins and stash them on the shelves without labels, or you will be kicking yourself the next time you need a screwdriver and you have to look through fifteen bins to find the one that contains your tools. Marking the outsides clearly with the contents makes retrieving what you need easy. Using the bin method may seem like another chore to do, but it will truly save you a great deal of time and money for years to come.

TIP #2: KNOW WHERE TO FIND YOUR IMPORTANT DOCUMENTS

You should be able to retrieve any important documents with ease. You can keep basic organization of these papers by using manila file folders, a marker (to label the top of each folder), and someplace to store where they can easily be retrieved. This is very helpful in having an organized home.

When you cannot find documents and important papers, you will end up wasting time calling people trying to get said documents re-sent to you repeatedly. Print, save, and file papers that you will need for the future. Your leasing or real-estate contracts, medical records, kid's school records, etc. should all be in file folders that are stored in either a filing cabinet or expanding file holders. This makes it easy to find essential documents when they are needed, saving you time and energy.

KEEP AND USE A SAFE

Every household should have a fireproof safe for storing the family's most important documents, such as wills, passports, and titles to homes and vehicles. (Speaking of wills, all parents should make it a priority to have a living will made. In the case of your untimely death, you want to be able to dictate in advance who will have custody of your children. If you don't yet have a living will, take the time to have one made immediately.)

Here is a list of some other items that should be kept in your fireproof safe:

- Titles to vehicles and other property that have ownership titles or deeds

- Passports

- Social security cards

- Insurance policies for your home

- Life insurance policy documents

- Birth certificates

- Jewelry appraisals

- Photos of your home, each room within the home, and the contents (in case this is ever needed for insurance or legal reasons)

Not all fireproof safes are waterproof. You may want to consider placing your important documents inside a waterproof document holder. You can find these types of containers for purchase online from a variety of manufacturers. Some of them are waterproof and fireproof certified.

SAVE USER'S MANUALS AND KEEP THEM IN ONE PLACE

Whenever we purchase a new appliance or a device that comes with an owner's manual, I file that manual in its home—a document-sized basket that I keep on an upper shelf in our laundry room. You never know when you may need to refer to the instruction manual for your laptop or your refrigerator, and even though most owner's manuals are available online, I find that having a physical document can be easier to read. Hanging on to these manuals is also helpful in the event that you decide to sell certain items in the future. Keeping all your manuals in one place means you'll know where to find them if you should need them.

Believe it or not, I don't alphabetize my owner's manuals. The basket is never filled so full that I can't scan through the contents within a couple of minutes when I need to find a particular manual. It isn't often that I refer to the owner's manuals, but, as I said, you never know when you might need to do so. For example, there was a default setting on our washing machine for an end-of-cycle beep that would sound every two minutes until we opened the washer door or pressed cancel. It was annoying, especially if I put in a load just before going to bed. The washing machine would beep all night long or until I got out of bed to press the cancel button. Thanks to the manual, I quickly figured out how to silence the end-of-cycle continuous beep feature.

Don't store your manuals in a prime real-estate location such as a kitchen drawer. Rather, keep that space saved for items you use on a daily or weekly basis, and stash your manuals deep in a closet or high on a shelf—clearly labeled, of course, so you can easily find them if and when you need them.

TIP #3: PICK UP AS YOU GO

It was my dad who taught me long ago that picking up as you go about your routine can save you from reaching the end of your day with a massive mess strewn about the entire house. It is far easier to pick things up and put them away throughout the day than to wait until day's end to tackle a huge, time-consuming mess. Modeling this method of cleaning up throughout the day to your kids teaches them a life skill that will serve them well far into the future, because nobody wants to be married to a slob who thinks nothing of throwing their PJs on the floor in the morning, leaving their towel on the bathroom vanity after showering, kicking off their shoes and draping their coat over the couch when they get home, or leaving their dinner dishes in the sink. Untidy habits make for an untidy home. Meanwhile, making a habit of tidying up throughout the day, as you use items and are finished with them, creates neatness and maintains order. If we can adopt this habit for ourselves, we can instill it in our kids.

 MAKE A HABIT OF TIDYING UP THROUGHOUT THE DAY. IF YOU ADOPT THIS HABIT FOR YOURSELF, YOU CAN INSTILL IT IN YOUR KIDS.

In our house, we have a rule that everyone puts his or her breakfast dishes in the dishwasher. This act requires just a little effort from each person, as opposed to the greater amount of effort and time that would be required if only one person had the task of loading all the dirty breakfast dishes. I can't emphasize enough how helpful it is to have picking up after oneself as a household rule!

In the same way, our household has an expectation that everyone stashes their own belongings when they return home from school or work. Make sure you have a designated spot for storing shoes, jackets, backpacks, purses, keys, and so forth. When everything has a home, it should not be too much to ask of your family members that they return every item to its rightful spot.

There are other daily habits that can prove helpful in keeping your home organized and tidy. I've made a list of examples below, so that you can consider making these steps part of your regular routine—and also asking your spouse and children to do the same. Remember, if you're going to break an old habit, such as dropping your shoes in the hall and throwing your coat over a chair when you get home, then you need to establish a new habit to replace it: stash your shoes on a rack in the closet, hang up your coat, and so forth. Here are some new habits to consider adopting as you get rid of old, untidy habits:

- When you use up a roll of toilet paper, replace it immediately.

- At the end of the day, hang up any clothes that you plan to wear again before washing; dirty clothes should go straight into the hamper.

- Make your bed and open the bedroom window shades every morning.

- Load dirty dishes into the dishwasher immediately after using them.

- Following a shower or bath, hang up damp towels immediately, and make sure each person has a designated hook so that towels don't get mixed up.

- Immediately following any bathroom preparations, tidy up the area by returning toothbrushes to their holder, putting any makeup or other toiletries back in drawers or storage bins, and so on. Once the countertop is clear, wipe it down in order to remove any residual soap, makeup, hair, etc. Nobody wants to come home to a sink smattered with hardened toothpaste globs coated in hair!

- Clean as you go. This policy is especially important after such activities as indoor play and meal preparation/cooking. Have your children put away the cars or dolls they were playing with before they take out any other toys. As you are cooking dinner, pick up as you go by putting away ingredients after you've used them, stashing away small appliances once they've done their job, and loading dirty mixing bowls and cutting boards into the dishwasher. This habit, applied to whatever you're doing, helps to keep your home tidier overall and prevents you and your family from facing a mountain of housework at the end of the day. (Having your children participate also ensures you won't be stuck with a mess after they go to bed.)

TIP #4: DECLUTTER AND DONATE

You should declutter your home on a daily basis instead of waiting for the mess to pile up before you tackle it. This doesn't mean you have to sort your junk drawer every day or organize your closets on a daily basis. What it *does* mean is that you make a habit of routinely getting rid of unused items. When you check the mail, sort everything immediately over your garbage can or recycle bin so you can immediately discard any junk mail. Don't lay the day's mail in a stack that accumulates into an enormous mound before you try going through it all. Do it as it comes, on a daily basis, and do it quickly. Making a habit of immediately discarding any junk is a big help in keeping your home clutter free.

Not everything needs to go in the trash. Designate a bin for items that can be donated or sold on consignment. I keep a plastic bin tucked in a corner of my closet for articles of clothing and accessories that I plan to give away. If I put on a garment and decide that it either no longer fits, is too worn, or no longer suits my style, I take it off and place it in the giveaway bin. If the item stays in the bin for several months without my ever changing my mind and retrieving it, then I pack it up for donation. I also keep a bin labeled "Donate" on a counter in our garage for household items I decide to donate. Having a place or "home" for items that my family no longer needs but that may be useful to others creates an easy system for setting aside items to donate in the future. I generally drop off a donation of items to a local charity once every few months.

TIP #5: DO A FINAL PICKUP BEFORE BED

I don't like waking up to a messy home. Knowing that my house is a wreck makes it harder for me to get up in the morning because I dread all the cleaning that awaits me. That's why I have long made it a habit to do one last pickup before I go to bed at night. This task became easier when the little humans living in my home grew capable of picking up after themselves and learned to make a habit of tidying throughout the day. They quickly figured out the truth that if everyone does their part during the day to keep things neat and organized, then the end-of-day picking-up process takes a lot less time and effort than it otherwise would.

Before I go to bed, I usually arrange the couch pillows the way I like them, load any remaining dishes into the dishwasher and start the cycle, and pick up any toys or other items that were left out after the kids went to bed. (Even though they're pretty good at picking up after themselves, it isn't uncommon for me to find a few stray items at the end of the day that need to be put away.) Then I shut off the lights, check that the doors are locked, and arm the security system. This final walk-through of the house must happen anyway for me to check that the doors are locked, and it does not require too much effort from me to put things in order along the way.

If your end-of-day pickup process takes you more than twenty minutes, it means the other people in your house are not doing what they should throughout the day. If you are finding yourself picking up piles of LEGOs, be sure to remind the kids the next day that it's their responsibility to clean them up next time. Alternatively, you could leave the LEGOs on the floor and simply wake your kids extra early the following morning so they can clean up their playthings before school. Most kids aren't keen on waking up early and will likely try harder to avoid this consequence in the future.

If my kids ever refuse to clean up a certain item they had been using, they forfeit that item for as long a time as I see fit. I might say to my daughter, for example, "You say you can't find your favorite shoes for school? Well, I guess you should have put them where they belong after school yesterday. You'll just have to wear a different pair of shoes to school today, and if you can show me that you know how to put your things away after school today, you can have your favorite shoes back tomorrow."

TIP #6: BE READY THE NIGHT BEFORE

One key to making sure your family starts each day on the right foot with as smooth a morning as possible is to lay out the night before everything you know you'll need the following day. I will discuss this tactic in greater detail later on, but most of us probably prefer getting out the door without any hassle and arriving at school and work on time. Starting each day rushing around, running behind the clock, and having to yell at or threaten our family members in order to get them out the door on time isn't any fun! One of the best ways to prepare for a smooth and punctual morning departure is to prepare as much as possible the night before, whether it's by choosing what to wear the next day, packing up briefcases and backpacks, prepping lunches, or something else.

Personally, I like to pick out my outfits the night before I plan to wear them. I never know what I am going to encounter in a given morning. I could have a child with a bloody nose, or I might need to help clean up a massive milk spill on the kitchen floor, or something else could happen that would demand valuable time I would have otherwise spent trying to figure out what to wear and getting myself ready. Planning my outfits in advance makes life easier for me because it frees me from worrying about what to wear in case there is some sort of crisis or even just a minor aberration from the normal morning routine that might derail my preparations. More often than not, I feel relieved and fortunate for having picked out my clothes and prepared my purse and other items the previous evening.

Another way I save time in the mornings is by doing my makeup on the go. I keep my everyday cosmetic products in a carryall bag that I take along when I drive the kids to school. Once I've dropped off the kids, I like to park and apply my makeup, all the while listening to music or an Audible book, before heading off to run errands or attend any meetings I may have scheduled. This routine saves me from having to parcel out time in the at-home routine for makeup, and it means I don't need to drive home after the daily school drop-off to "put on my face" before heading out again.

Assembling my personal items the night before makes it look like I spent more time getting ready in the morning than I actually did. I will lay out my clothes, accessories, and shoes. I also usually lay out a hat in case I don't have time to do my hair. For some reason, wearing a hat seems to give people the impression that I spent more time getting ready than I actually did. Laying out a coordinated outfit the night before helps me look well put together without having to make time to do it in the morning. I don't like to get up any earlier than I must. My brain takes a little while to wake up, so my ability to pick out a well-coordinated outfit is better in the evening than in early morning hours.

Even if I were a morning person, I would still prepare my things the night before. It gives me extra motivation to get out of bed, because I look forward to putting on whatever I coordinated and laid out the previous night. Knowing that, for example, my Bible study homework is completed and the workbook is waiting on the counter, along with a gift I plan on taking to a friend, all ready to be picked up when I head out for the day helps my mornings go more smoothly. I stay literally two steps ahead of myself by preparing the night before. I may not be able to prevent a child from dumping his entire bowl of cereal on the floor at breakfast, but I can make it possible for me to put minimal effort and time into getting ready in the morning by doing as much as I can the night before. My nightly routine usually includes showering, since I never know when a sudden disaster might divert my ability to shower in the morning.

The goal of preparing the night before is to give yourself at shot at having an enjoyable morning that isn't rushed or crazed. The way your day starts out sets the tone for your entire day. Give yourself a better shot at getting out the door on time and being prepared for the day by having everything prepared and laid out the night before.

AN ORGANIZED LIFE

Having an organized life is also an important aspect of being a parent who manages time to the best of my abilities. It allows for all the work that I am doing to fall into place as planned, and for my successes to shine through. For me, organized planning is a key to success in every endeavor.

When the COVID-19 pandemic struck, our kids' school shut down for a time, and our family made the decision to homeschool. Of course, my approach to this endeavor started with organization. Without a plan, our homeschooling efforts would have ended in disaster. We did not homeschool by choice but because of the temporary closure of our local school district due to the COVID-19 pandemic. Maybe your family experienced a similar challenge. Our kids were nearing the end of spring break when we were told that their school would be on hold for a while. No end date was provided for this new situation, so I decided to approach homeschooling as if we were going to continue with it for the remainder of the school year. Had I elected in advance to homeschool my kids, the planner in me would probably have taken an entire summer to select the curriculum, arrange a schedule, and order the necessary materials. But I didn't have a summer to plan; I had only one weekend. Therefore, I knew that while I needed to put a plan in place and create a schedule, it would be necessary to leave room for flexibility as we progressed.

My first step was to consider the subjects being covered at school so I would know what we needed to cover at home. The subjects were essentially our overall goals. I wanted to ensure that my kids would be picking up where they'd left off and would continue learning at their own grade level. For example, in second-grade math, my daughter had just finished learning subtraction with regrouping and had started exploring multiplication. We picked up where her school lessons had left off and moved forward from there. Next, I looked for materials. I found workbooks on Amazon by grade and subject. I also sought out websites and apps that we could use to supplement my teachings. Once I knew which subjects we were doing, then we got a schedule going.

Our first schedule was a draft that I typed on my laptop, with subjects organized by half-hour increments from nine in the morning until two in the afternoon, building in time for lunch and several breaks. I knew that the schedule would need to be revised as we went along, so I kept my laptop open on the kitchen counter and made regular adjustments to the schedule.

The first major change to our schedule occurred when I found out about a local woman offering free online art classes at ten in the morning, Monday through Friday. My kids participated in class the first day and were very engaged. The format was fun and encouraged creativity. I added the art class to our daily schedule and shifted the timing of some other subjects to make room for it.

By the end of our first week of homeschooling, after making several modifications, I had come up with a schedule I believed would adequately support our homeschooling goals. We printed out the schedule and posted it in the kitchen to keep ourselves on task each day, but it didn't take long for my kids to know the schedule by heart. The schedule helped keep them focused because they knew that none of their lessons or worksheets would go on forever; each one had a concrete time slot. Kids thrive with schedules and order.

Along the same lines, children function best when they know what is expected of them. Making the expected time commitment clear, along with clearly outlining the learning objectives and assignments that are to be completed during that time frame, creates a peaceful learning environment. My kids didn't complain about doing any specific subjects, nor did they whine and demand more breaks. They knew when each subject would be covered during the day and for how long; they also knew when to expect breaks and meals. Having a familiar schedule helped them understand the process for our homeschool classroom and prepared them for what we were doing, step-by-step, for the entire day.

For our family, homeschooling—even though it wasn't something I had ever intended on doing—was successful because we made a clear plan and followed it consistently. The broad goals we had set were broken down into daily tasks arranged according to a schedule that ensured they would complete what the school district expected of them. Having a plan that was clear, reasonable, and achievable made our homeschooling process successful. I won't pretend that we didn't encounter any bumps in the road or experience any failures along the way. We anticipated those things happening, and when they did, we made the necessary adjustments, then proceeded with our plan.

Homeschooling didn't just fall into place for us. It was a matter of planning, preparation, and scheduling. The same is true for just about every area of life. If we think that success will just fall into our laps without our forming an actual plan to achieve success, then we are deluded and fooling ourselves. *When we identify a goal, we need to create a plan that will enable us to achieve that goal.* Leaving it all to chance will rarely result in what we were hoping for. But when we identify a goal, anticipate the work we'll need to do to reach it, and then divide up that work into smaller, achievable tasks on a realistic schedule, we set ourselves up for success.

ACHIEVING GOALS IN AN ORGANIZED MANNER

Being well-organized significantly improves our chances of working productively and achieving success. We (1) set a goal, (2) break down that goal into specific tasks that support the overall goal, and then (3) draft a schedule or timetable that allows us to plan how to get everything done. These three steps provide us with a path to success. We may say that we want to lose twenty pounds, but that weight loss is not going to happen magically. We need to create a specific plan that includes a timetable or schedule. For example, we could break down the goal of losing twenty pounds into the smaller goals of, say, losing five pounds per month for four months, or losing a pound per week for twenty weeks. Next, we would create a plan for losing those pounds. We may research diets and weight-loss plans that sound feasible to us, avoiding any gimmick diets or weight-loss plans promising instant losses of major amounts. We would decide on a plan that we believed we could stick with for the long haul, crafting a complementary exercise regimen that we could commit to. The goal of losing twenty pounds becomes much more realistic when we have an organized plan of attack. With intentional meal planning, daily workouts, and an overall schedule, we create an atmosphere of organization that enables us to fulfill short-term goals leading to the achievement of a larger, long-term goal.

Far too many people approach life without making any organizational plans. Simply saying, "I want to lose twenty pounds, so I am going to exercise more and eat better" may sound like a good plan, but it is not enough. Only an organized approach that plans out the entire process, from first to final pound, will result in the weight loss you want to achieve. The "What," "When," and "How" need to be specified in advance, for meals and exercise alike.

ONLY AN ORGANIZED APPROACH THAT PLANS OUT THE ENTIRE PROCESS WILL RESULT IN THE ACHIEVEMENT OF A PARTICULAR GOAL.

Just as happened with our family's homeschooling plan, you may need to reassess your weight-loss plans and make adjustments along the way, especially in the beginning. You may set your sights on working out five days a week, only to discover that your muscles need a day to recover after you've done a weightlifting workout or an intense cardiovascular class. Recovery days are important for athletes, and they're essential for anyone working toward weight loss with exercise. You may need to dial down your pace and give your body time to rest and rebuild muscle. Making adjustments is not the same as giving up or throwing away the plan. It is only through modifications, especially in the early phases of your plan, that you will find a plan that will work for you for the duration of your journey.

If you draft an organizational plan for an area of your life that you are dead-set on following to a tee, you may be defeating yourself before you even get started. Allow yourself some flexibility in your planning. For example, if you want to start eating more home-cooked meals in an effort to be healthier, set up a plan that gives you the space and flexibility to eat out or order takeout if the need arises. Making your meals from scratch seven days a week might be too lofty a goal. If you aren't accustomed to doing much cooking, it's likely that, by day three, you'll be exhausted, and your house will be a mess because you've spent so much time in your (also messy) kitchen that other housework isn't getting done. You may need to revise your plan a bit to facilitate long-term success. If your overall goal is to eat less fast food, then maybe you need to give a little on the idea that every meal must be made from scratch. The occasional healthy premade meal from your local grocery store may help you achieve your goal. You can incorporate this type of meal into your menu rotation once or twice a week so that you won't overwhelm yourself by attempting to cook everything from scratch. Again, the key is having a plan that leaves room for revisions, especially as you are getting started. You may have more realistic expectations once you've gotten a few days or weeks under your belt.

Having an organized life involves setting goals and making detailed plans to achieve those goals. Setting goals that are *realistic* is every bit as important as allowing for revisions to the schedule you have vowed to follow as you pursue those goals. When we find that a schedule or plan is not working, many times, we end up throwing in the towel and quitting altogether. But if we opt for a mindset that brings flexibility to the process, especially when we are just starting out and still learning what it will take to achieve our goals, we are likelier to stick to our revised goals and to fulfill them. No flexibility often leads to zero outcome. Set those goals, but also allow yourself to revise those goals and modify the schedule as you get into it, so that you create a flexible, working plan that is more likely to be achieved in the long run.

CHAPTER 4:

LET GO OF PERFECT

You know what is a huge drain on your time? Always trying to do things perfectly. If I am good at one thing, it may very well be letting go of perfect and calling things "good enough." I have had other moms call me a perfectionist. That's just because people see what they want to see. Usually, those who perceive me as "perfect" are friends and family members who are particularly fond of me. But, believe me, I receive plenty of reminders about my lack of perfection—for example, the emails I've received regarding improper punctuation in a blog post of mine or a typo in an article I published. Those searching for flaws can easily find them because I am not perfect. I prefer to take the "good enough" approach and keep moving forward.

Taking the "good enough" approach, as opposed to the pursuit of perfection, frees up a great deal of time and mental energy. Striving for perfection in any area of life is like chasing rainbows with the hopes of catching one—it won't happen. For us as humans, perfection is unattainable. There are bound to be at least minor errors and flaws found in anything and everything we do, including raising kids and managing a household. If you've tended toward perfectionism in the past, change your perspective on perfect by accepting the fact that perfect isn't realistic, and make "good enough" your new mantra.

WHEN THE PURSUIT OF PERFECTION BECOMES AN EXCUSE

For many people, the pursuit of perfection turns into an excuse to not even try to do something because of the feeling of being bound to fail. I used to avoid cooking because I thought, *If I can't prepare amazingly delicious, perfect meals all the time, then cooking must not be my thing.* I would simply tell people, "I don't cook." We often give up on something before we even really try because we think that if we can't expect to do it perfectly, then we shouldn't do it at all. Such a belief hinders our ability to be and to do, on many levels. My giving up on cooking before putting any effort into trying it was a prime of example of a defeatist attitude. The truth is, just because I can't prepare every meal to perfection doesn't mean I shouldn't give it my best shot. Just like with any skill, there is a learning curve. Creating great meals comes once you've mastered making more basic meals. You become decent, or "good enough," at preparing certain basic recipes, and then you can move up to more advanced or complicated recipes. They say that Rome wasn't built in a day, and neither was any chef's recipe repertoire. Don't decide something isn't worth trying and give up because you fear imperfect results. You don't have to be the "best cook in the world" to feed your family nutritious, tasty meals. Just look for "good enough" recipes as a starting point and expand from there.

 DON'T DECIDE SOMETHING ISN'T WORTH TRYING AND GIVE UP BECAUSE YOU FEAR IMPERFECT RESULTS.

Our skills build upon themselves. We shouldn't give up on doing something because we can't do it perfectly and won't be the best at it. Sometimes, we throw in the towel before really trying because we don't want to start at the bottom. We sign up for an art class expecting to paint like Monet on our first attempt. We sign up for golf lessons thinking we'll turn into Tiger Woods overnight. But most learned skills don't work like that. Having a natural bent or ability for doing something can help, but most skills require us to practice for months or years to attain the level we desire. Whatever we would like to do, we can't expect perfection or a high level of expertise when we are just getting started. We must set realistic expectations so that we can give ourselves a chance to get started and then build on our skills. You won't be perfect when you get started—and you won't be perfect even when you've honed a skill as much as you can! Just don't use that fact as an excuse to prevent you from even trying.

THROW AWAY "PERFECT" AND LET YOUR CREATIVITY BLOSSOM

When you decide that you are going to throw away a pursuit of absolute perfection, you give yourself permission to try new things, or maybe to do familiar things in a different way. You will unlock your potential for creativity when you no longer subscribe to the notion that things have to be done a certain way.

When I finally conceded that I didn't have to be a perfect chef in order for my family to enjoy my culinary creations, it opened the door for me to discover new recipes and different ways of doing things. I dropped the belief that I had to cook every meal completely from scratch. Who says you can't call a pie homemade if you used a premade crust and canned apple filling? Anyone who would criticize your use of such ingredients probably isn't a true friend. (I am only half-joking.) A true friend will say, "Of course, it's homemade. You assembled the ingredients and baked it at home." Using "shortcuts" in the kitchen is *not* cheating; it is a means of saving time and effort, thereby making your culinary goals more attainable. Do you think you'd have to pick the apples from the tree yourself for your pie to classify as homemade? Where does this necessity for doing everything ourselves end, so that we can get more done in a day? Drop the notion that you need to do it all from scratch. Give up the idea that if you can't do every step on your own, it isn't worth doing. Make that apple pie, and feel free to use a premade crust and canned filling! Your family will appreciate a pie, whether you made it entirely from scratch, used premade ingredients, or purchased the pie from a bakery.

Taking the "good enough" approach to areas where we normally would have chased after perfection protects our sanity and helps us to invest our greatest time and effort where they really count. For example, let's say you signed up to provide the decorations for your child's class party celebrating Valentine's Day. Does that mean you're expected to scour Pinterest for hours and end up sewing your own buntings and creating handmade centerpieces for every table? Of course not. Now, if that type of project would bring you joy, and you have the time for it, then, by all means, proceed! But if you opt for adding homemade decorations to an already lengthy to-do list because you think it's the only way of being the "perfect mom," then it's time to change your thinking. Store-bought streamers and premade paper hearts will be just as appreciated by a classroom full of kids as homemade decorations that were labored over for ten-plus hours. Don't fall into the trap of feeling that you must be a DIY perfectionist parent. Again, if you enjoy doing homemade projects and you have the time for them, then go for it. But if you opt for the DIY route because you believe doing so will earn you accolades or special recognition of some sort, then you may want to consider changing your approach.

JUST TRY IT

When you let go of the illusion that anything can be done perfectly, you give yourself permission to move forward and try it out. If you are tied to the belief that the only way you can start a project or begin doing something new is if you think you can be successful and do it perfectly, then you are severely limiting your ability to try new things.

 IF WE WILL EMBRACE THE POSSIBILITY OF FAILURE, SEEING IT AS AN OPPORTUNITY FOR LEARNING AND IMPROVING, THEN WE ARE SUCCEEDING ALREADY.

When you fear that you will not be "good enough," you often keep yourself from trying at all. But if you let go of any expectations and allow yourself to try with no strings attached, you are unleashing yourself. You are giving yourself permission to try something, even if it involves a failure (or two or ten). If we resist trying something new because we fear being less than perfect—or, worse, because we refuse to allow a potential failure to enter into the picture—we are killing our potential. But if we'll embrace the possibility of failure, seeing it as an opportunity for learning and improving, then we are succeeding already.

Set your expectations a little lower, and, if it's oil painting you're trying, don't be devastated if your first project isn't gallery worthy. You will probably create many canvases that you consider failures before you attain a result you find satisfying. Even the most renowned of painters has trashed plenty of projects! But they never would have created the masterpieces they're known for if they had never tried and failed, and tried again. Give yourself permission to be less than perfect. Failure must also be a possibility you are willing to entertain for the sake of success in the long run. Most great successes are the result of someone practicing persistence and ultimately overcoming repeated failure.

HOW TO ESCAPE THE TRAP OF PERFECTIONISM

If you find yourself insisting on perfection in every area, and you see the wisdom in ceasing this striving, consider the following tips to remove yourself from the pointless race toward something that is truly unachievable for us in this life.

RECOGNIZE THE IMPRESSION OF PERFECTION AS AN ILLUSION

Most of us can probably think of someone we long thought of—or maybe even still think of—as being perfect. We need to intentionally burst the bubble of this impression whenever it forms in our minds. Growing up, I loved watching the Miss America Pageant on television. The young women representing each state were not only beautiful; they poured their energies into charity work, possessed amazing talents, touted major academic accomplishments, and were heading down a path to certain personal and career successes. To me, each of those fifty women appeared perfect. Guess what? That was an illusion. Those women had struggles and problems just like the rest of us.

Nobody is immune to problems, failures, or troubles—not even the most polished-looking of individuals. That classroom mom with her immaculate outfits, beautifully coiffed hair, well-dressed kids, and show-stopping homemade desserts may have an eating disorder or a shopping addiction. That neighbor with her athlete's physique and successful career may harbor depression or anxiety. You never know what someone else may be dealing with. Everyone has a personal struggle of some sort. And even if there isn't a major issue someone is dealing with, nobody is without a sin nature, so we all have flaws. The next time you start picturing someone else as perfect and envying her for it, stop yourself and remind yourself that you aren't seeing the entire picture. People are like icebergs; we see only what is above the surface. There may be a world of other issues going on—including trials, difficulties, failures— hidden from view. All of us know the effort of concealing our major imperfections when we present ourselves to the public eye. So, don't be fooled by those perfect-looking parents and families. The appearance of perfection is an illusion, and the better we are able to remember this, the more grace we can give ourselves—and others.

STOP COMPARING YOURSELF TO OTHERS

We need to stop comparing ourselves to others. The only person we should use for the purposes of comparison is ourselves. When you attend events for moms and their kids, such as a library story hour, or even when you're out shopping, do you find yourself constantly sizing up the other mothers you see and comparing their wardrobes with your own? Do you dwell on feelings of self-pity because you wish that you had better clothes, a nicer purse, or more time to get ready in the mornings? Do you feel as if you're failing in some way because you see another mom at the playground who looks more put-together and poised than you think you look? If you regularly have these sorts of thoughts going through your mind, you need to retrain your brain. Remember, you don't know what's really going on in the lives of the mothers you see when you're out and about. They may be emotional train wrecks who are simply lipsticked on the outside in order to look put-together. They may or may not have it together, but one thing is sure: everyone has struggles to deal with. Never assume that someone's ability to come across as put-together is proof that she doesn't have any issues. *Everyone* has issues, and we are all trying to deal with them as best we can. If you see a mom whose appearance you admire, then go ahead and pay her a compliment. Goodness knows how much we mothers value words of affirmation, especially when our children are little and we hardly have the time to get ourselves ready for the day! And you never know when a compliment from someone else will make your day. You can make someone else's day by paying that person a genuine compliment. Making a habit of looking for things to compliment about other people—whether it's an aspect of their appearance or a character trait—trains us to search for the good in others rather than closing ourselves off from them in feelings of envy or self-pity. It also just might lead to some new friendships for you and your kids!

EMBRACE THE MESS

I have some mom friends who don't permit Play-Doh, Slime, Kinetic Sand, and other "messy" play items in their homes. They claim that these materials are just too messy, and they don't want them in their house. Believe me, I can understand their perspective; I like to have my own house picked up and looking clean and shiny. But, let's face it: a home where people actually live will be messy, to some degree. We need to accept the mess as part of life, even if we clean it up as we go (and add a spray of Lysol once the kids are in bed). Especially if you homeschool or have little ones at home all day, some messiness is inevitable. This mess is proof that life exists in your home! And removing any item that might create a mess is not a realistic approach. Whether your kids prefer Play-Doh, LEGOs, wooden blocks, or something else, there's bound to be a mess when these playthings are in use. Try to bring yourself to a place of being okay with this mess. It isn't permanent; it's a state of living. Your children would rather have a patient parent who allows some flexibility in messes than one who becomes upset, nagging, or angry when a mess occurs.

We allow our families to live in our home, and this means we must allow them to make a mess when needed. Of course, we should enlist their help in the cleanup of said mess; but when we set overly lofty expectations for a clean and tidy home, we impede our family's ability to live. Allow your family to live and thrive by keeping yourself from getting upset when messes happen as the result of play and everyday life. Hold your children accountable for cleaning up their messes when they are done playing or creating, but don't allow messes to cause you or your family members anxiety because you have set the bar too high when it comes to keeping a tidy home.

CALL IT DONE

Do you tend to fuss over projects once they're complete, trying to improve them even further in hopes of making them "perfect"? One unnecessary activity that robs you of time you could have spent on other worthy pursuits is continuing to work on a task that has already been completed. Let's say you bake a batch of cupcakes for your daughter's preschool class, and after you frost them, you decide that they look a little sad—so you feel compelled to start over and make a brand-new batch. Do you really think that your daughter and her peers are going to judge you or reject your cupcakes for being "less than perfect"? As we discussed earlier, it's healthy to reach a place of being okay with something less than perfection. And as long as there's just as much sugar as flour in the recipe, those kids will probably love the cupcakes—even if the treats don't look like they were made in a five-star bakery. Those preschoolers aren't familiar with the recipe you followed; they won't be comparing the appearance to the corresponding photo you found on

Pinterest. It is the act of comparing with what was being aimed for that makes "Pinterest Fails" so funny. But without a standard of comparison, it is unlikely that anyone will criticize your cupcakes, and I highly doubt that anybody would turn down a homemade treat on the basis of appearance. What matters most is the love and care for your child that were the reason you baked those cupcakes in the first place. Trust me, your daughter and her peers will devour the treats, even if they aren't "Pinterest worthy."

For most projects, once you've finished, it's best not to fixate on aspects that could have been done better or the things you could have improved. When the task is complete, move on. Otherwise, you are likely to waste countless minutes or hours redoing satisfactory work that you have already completed.

Perfectionists tend to have a hard time calling something done, and they may redo their work repeatedly. All this extra work may or may not improve the end result, but it has claimed a great deal of their time. Reclaim your time by being satisfied with your work rather than insisting on a redo when the outcome is not "perfect." Does the flower arrangement you prepare and deliver to a healing friend need to be perfectly arranged, or can it be good enough? Do you need to toil over gift-wrapping your spouse's birthday gift, using high-quality paper and lots of fancy ribbon so the effect is picture-perfect, or can you use some tissue paper and a gift bag and call it done?

If you insist on completing each and every project to the highest standards possible, you will find yourself finishing few projects. Many of your endeavors will stall out because you can't reach a point of thinking they are good enough. You will tell yourself, *I'll just come back later and do it again*, but you will end up procrastinating indefinitely because you are afraid the finished product won't be good enough. My question is: Good enough for whom? Your own perfectionist tendencies? Let it go. Get the project to a place of being "good enough" and then call it done so that you can move on to other things. You will save yourself time and energy by being satisfied with even a "less-than-perfect" job, and you'll be freed and energized for the next project.

PERFECTION, EXCELLENCE, AND GETTING IT DONE

I hope you don't think I'm discouraging having high standards and striving toward excellence. Excellence is *not* the same as perfection. Make sure that you make an accurate distinction between the two in your mind. Setting standards for yourself and your family is a wise practice, especially when it comes to morals, values, and the like. However, a constant pursuit of "excellence" (perfection) in all areas of life is an impossible goal that will only impose stress on you and your family. You must decide, sometimes on the fly, the areas in which pursuing excellence is worthwhile, versus the areas in which getting the job done to a satisfactory degree is enough. If you demand excellence in every area, you are going to cause burnout for yourself and your kids.

 IF YOU DEMAND EXCELLENCE IN EVERY AREA, YOU ARE GOING TO CAUSE BURNOUT FOR YOURSELF AND YOUR KIDS.

In our household, we prioritize academic excellence over excellence in sports. When it comes to athletics, we encourage our kids to work hard and try their best, but we do not demand excellence. If we were to pressure our kids to excel to the same degree that they do with their schoolwork in sports, household chores, behavior, and so forth, this wholesale burden would likely break them.

Too many kids are getting burned out—physically, mentally, and emotionally—by the time they reach high school because of the pressure of their families' overly lofty expectations. It is good to set standards and encourage a striving for excellence in all areas, but it is unrealistic to *expect* an outcome of excellence in all areas.

We need to let our kids know that it's okay to participate in something even if they don't win a trophy or score a medal. If we act disappointed when our children don't finish in first place or set a new school record, we are setting them up for emotional failure. Ease off the pressure and give your kids a chance to set and work toward their own goals. Remind them (and remind yourself) that doing their best is all that matters, and never let them think that they're letting you down if they don't do something "perfectly." You've heard it before: winning isn't everything. Make sure you live out this motto as an example to your kids, so they see the truth of it for themselves.

YOU DON'T HAVE TO BE PERFECT TO BE AMAZING

Some of us fall into the trap of believing that nothing short of perfection makes our pursuits worthwhile. The truth is that we can do amazing things and achieve great accomplishments even if our efforts aren't anywhere near perfect. God made us unique and special. Nobody else in the world is quite like you, which means nobody can do things just like you do them. Embrace the creation that God has made you to be, and take pride in the amazing things you're able to do, imperfect though they may be. You are worthy because God made you to be you!

"JUST DO THE NEXT THING THAT MUST GET DONE"

Raising kids and running a household can be exhausting. When I had just had our twins, I thought that it was just a phase of exhaustion during their infancy and that things would get easier as they grew older.

I'm not sure whether that was just what I needed to tell myself in order to cope at the time or whether I was delusional. Either way, I was wrong. As the kids got older (the twins are now six and our daughter is eight), I found that life did not become any easier, only different. I still have the same amount of work to do on any given day: laundry, cooking, cleaning, school drop-off and pick-up, helping kids with homework, after-school sports, and any career-related tasks. All that is on top of the effort it takes to get myself ready in the morning, respond to emails, make necessary phone calls...the list goes on and on. I sometimes wonder how it all gets done in a day. (Well, to be honest, some days it does, and some days it doesn't!)

There are certainly days when I can't possibly tackle every item on my list. So, I order my list according to urgency, and I address the most pressing tasks first. I call this "just doing the next thing that must get done." If you were to visit my home for more than a day, you would probably hear me saying aloud to myself, "Just do the next thing that must get done." I think of this phrase when I feel overwhelmed because there isn't enough time to get it all done and I have hit a wall of exhaustion. I often find myself using this phrase at the end of a busy day when I am already tired by the time I pick up the kids from school and I still have things to accomplish before bed, especially when I just want to go home, unwind, and relax (i.e., sit on the couch and binge-watch a purely entertaining show). Such a scenario is usually not an option. The kids need transportation to their after-school activities. Dinner needs to be made. The kids need my help with their homework. And, by the way, the dog just puked in the other room. It is in these situations that I tell myself, "Just do the next thing that must get done." Obviously, cleaning up after the dog is priority number one; putting off cleanup till later will only mean more work because the mess will have set into the carpet. Anything I can clean up immediately will save me from having a more difficult mess to clean up later. Once I've cleaned up that mess, I tell myself again, "Just do the next thing that must get done."

I find that when I use this phrase, I tend to simplify my tasks. I don't make extra work for myself, nor do I make tasks any more complicated than they need to be. For example, instead of making a big production over dinner, I always have the option of heating a frozen pizza in the oven and pulling a premade salad from the refrigerator. Complicated meals have their place and time, but, for our family, weeknights aren't that time. Making use of store-bought meals helps make dinner preparation more manageable for me. Once the pizza is in the oven, I tell myself yet again, "Just do the next thing that must get done." On this particular night, the twins have lacrosse practice. While the pizza is cooking, I have the twins get changed for practice and put their gear by the door. That way, we will be ready to leave after we finish dinner.

In this situation, I may have a sewing project laid out that I had intended to complete that night and clean laundry piled up, waiting to be folded. I can ignore those tasks for this evening, focusing only on the things that *must* be done. Feeding my family dinner is more important than finishing the sewing project. The laundry will always be there; it is never ending. Skipping it on this particular evening is freeing, because I know I'll have several hours open in the morning after I drop the kids off at school the following day. Giving myself some flexibility also gives me more peace and contentment. As long as I've accomplished the tasks that absolutely had to get done on a given day, everything else—all other projects—can fall by the wayside temporarily.

There may be days or seasons when we experience exhausting days more often than not. One of the most tiring seasons is when you have babies and young children at home—little humans who wear you out with their constant need for help. If you spend most of your energy keeping those little people fed, clothed, and safe, please give yourself some slack. Keep doing the next "must-do" item on the list, and once the kids are in bed, you get some rest, too. Some days will be conducted more in survival mode than thriving mode. That's okay. Give yourself grace and flexibility. One day, you might feel like Super-Mom, with everything falling into place; the next day, you might find yourself in survival mode. Either way, it's okay. We all have both kinds of days. Just focus on doing the next thing you need to do.

CHAPTER 5:

DELEGATE

One of the biggest wastes of time in a household is the parents shouldering all the work. Delegation is key: it preserves your own energy and teaches your children responsibility. Children can be assigned chores from a very young age. If they can walk and talk, they are capable of doing more household jobs than you probably think. Some of the first chores you can delegate to them include making their beds in the morning, picking up their belongings, helping to load and unload the dishwasher, collect bags of garbage from smaller trash cans, dust, and even sweep the floors. Never underestimate the abilities of your children. And don't be surprised if your kids insist on helping and appear to take joy from the tasks they're doing! Most young children embrace any activity that seems usually reserved for adults, and they feel a sense of pride when they learn a new skill and start to master it.

Make sure that the members of your household know what duties are expected of them. Create a chore chart for your children, using pictures to illustrate the various jobs until your kids learn to read, at which point you can write out the jobs. When your children can refer to a chart and complete their daily chores without having to ask you what they're supposed to do, it saves you a lot of time and effort. Of course, an investment of time is required when you begin using a chore chart—you will need to demonstrate for your children how to perform their various assignments and then supervise their work, to a degree—but after a little practice, they will soon be able to do their daily tasks independently from you. Using an allowance or another type of reward system can help this routine fall into place more easily. Kids are glad to get with the program when they know what is expected of them and are aware of the rewards, and the consequences, for either completing or failing to complete their chores.

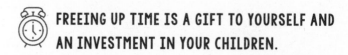 **FREEING UP TIME IS A GIFT TO YOURSELF AND AN INVESTMENT IN YOUR CHILDREN.**

For every chore that another person in the household completes instead of you yourself, you gain more time to tackle your own projects.

Freeing up time is a gift to yourself. You are also investing in your children, equipping them to become better, more self-sufficient human beings by giving them roles and responsibilities in the home.

Another way to delegate, if you have the means, is to hire outside help, such as a babysitter on certain evenings or a maid service that cleans your home once or twice a month. Paying for outside help is not a sign of weakness; it is a way of striking a balance that keeps the household running smoothly and harmoniously. Assess your financial situation and see whether this type of delegation may benefit you and your schedule.

DON'T BE A SLAVE

No single person should be doing it all, sacrificing their own well-being for the sake of their family members. If there are other humans over the age of two living in your home, they need to participate in the household chores.

Far too many parents end up shouldering the bulk of the housework. Some do this intentionally, because they don't want to "burden" their kids with too much work. They may feel that their kids have enough on their plates between homework, sports, and after-school activities. The problem with not expecting kids to help out around the house is threefold. Number one: it creates more work for the parents. If kids aren't helping out at all, then the entirety of the work falls on the shoulders of their parents, robbing the parents of energy and quality time that should be spent with their children. Number two: when kids aren't expected to do any chores, they take for granted all that their parents do around the home and end up feeling entitled. Number three: when kids aren't assigned chores, they aren't building key life competencies, such as the basics of cooking, how to clean bathrooms, how to do laundry, and so forth. You do your kids a disservice if you send them out into the world without at least a basic competence in the basic household tasks.

You are not a slave to your spouse or your children. If you have been toiling like a slave, doing all the work for everybody else, then stop! Decide which household tasks can be delegated—especially to your children—and start making assignments. Your kids need to learn the basics of cleaning, cooking, organizing, and laundry every bit as much as they need to learn arithmetic, history, and other areas of academic study.

EVERYONE HAS A PART TO PLAY

Every person who lives in a particular home should take part in the household chores. All of us have various skills and levels of ability, but everybody can help out, regardless of age. Tasks should be assigned according to ability, but make sure you challenge your kids with jobs of increasing complexity as they grow. My kids started making their beds as soon as they had transitioned from toddler beds to twin-size beds. At first, I simply asked them to pull up their covers and place their pillows at the head of the bed. The result wasn't perfect; to be honest, the beds often didn't look nice and neat, even though they were made. But the important thing was that my children were developing a habit that could be honed and improved upon. It's crucial to train our kids from an early age to take care of their own space through daily habits.

My kids know that having a space of their own is a privilege that comes with certain responsibilities. Our policy is that they start every day by making their beds and opening their window shades. They also know that we expect them to keep their toys put away, not left on the floor. These standards are helping our kids develop habits that contribute to our household values of tidiness and order—values that will serve them well as they grow and move out on their own.

ASSIGNING CHORES

Chores are assigned household duties. Most kids need to be assigned household chores if the parents expect their participation in the house-work. If you think your kids are going to volunteer to help out of a sense of duty, you may be waiting a long time. Granted, there are kids who relish running the vacuum cleaner or dusting the furniture, but they are as rare as unicorns. Even if your children show interest in learning a particular skill and helping with a task, that interest is bound to be short-lived unless you make the chore into a daily expectation.

Assigning specific chores to your kids, along with a time frame in which those chores are to be completed, makes it clear what is expected of your children in terms of helping around the house. If you merely tell them, "Your job is to keep the bathrooms clean," but you don't tell them how often they need to clean and what steps that cleaning process entails, then your bathrooms aren't likely to stay very clean.

Most kids require very specific instructions and a way of knowing when they should complete the chore. For example, if I want to put my daughter in charge of cleaning her bathroom, then I need to add that job to her chore chart. I might put it on the list of items to be completed every Saturday, and under the chore title, I would write out such sub-categories as: scrub the toilet, Windex the mirror, wipe down the coun-tertop and sink, scrub the bathtub, and mop the floor. This list makes it clear what I expect her to do when she cleans her bathroom, as well as when I expect her to do it.

More important than putting your children's chores on a chart is teaching your children how to do those chores correctly and safely. In order to teach my daughter how to clean her bathroom, I had her work alongside me as we cleaned two other bathrooms in our home. I talked her through every step and pointed out any key tips, like scrubbing the corners of the shower and making sure to wipe down the back and sides of the commode. Then I sent her to her own bathroom with the cleaning supplies and let her try it for herself.

Like any skill, cleaning a bathroom or doing laundry are tasks that your kids will need to practice in order to become proficient. Don't expect them to do a perfect job the first time they complete an assigned chore. Make sure you affirm their efforts and show appreciation for their contribution to the good of the household. In time, they'll be cleaning, cooking, and doing laundry like pros!

THE CHART METHOD

One morning, I was watching an episode of *Today*, and TV personalities Jenna Bush Hager and Sheinelle Jones were discussing the technique of bribing one's children. Both women admitted to resorting to the tactic of bribery when they felt it was needed. I was all ears, because what parent hasn't used bribery and wondered whether it was okay? Jenna Bush Hager described a time when her daughter came into her room extremely early in the morning, well before Jenna was ready to get up, and she told her daughter she would get ice cream later that morning if she went back to bed. I could completely relate! With a six-year-old daughter and four-year-old twin boys, I felt that I had been resorting to bribery—or threatening consequences for unwanted behavior—too often.

It didn't take me long to develop a form of "bribery," if you want to call it that, that we find extremely effective. It's the CHART method—a simple reward system that you can begin using with your kids today.

With this method, parents reward their children with toys, treats, and fun activities *when the children earn them*. It starts with a chart that has either 30 or 50 boxes to fill with check marks as the kids earn them. The completion of an entire chart is rewarded with whatever you and your kids agree on at the outset. Be sure to select a reward that your child really wants. My kids started with 30-box charts, and when they had filled the charts with check marks, they got to go shopping at Walmart or Target and select any toy priced beneath a specific dollar amount.

The first shopping trip like this that we made, you would have thought I was giving them each a million dollars. They were ecstatic! That's because they were in control of choosing exactly what they wanted. They also had control over when they earned their reward, because the redemption date depended on their own behavior. The CHART method specifies clear expectations for the kids while also giving parents the flexibility to offer kids the option of earning check marks.

I would recommend starting your kids on the smaller, 30-box chart. That way, they have fewer steps to a reward the first time around. For kids five and under, stick with the 30-box chart until they reach six years of age. Younger children need to receive rewards more frequently in order for the CHART system to work with them.

You can print a free copy of the CHART system with either 50 or 30 boxes from my website. Simply go to http://livingjoydaily. com/2018/07/02/yes-bribery-can-be-good-parenting-heres-how/, or go to www.livingjoydaily.com and type in "chart method" in the website's search bar.

The CHART acronym specifies the categories in which your kids can earn check marks:

C = Chores daily

H = Hygiene

A = Acting as asked

R = Reading

T = Time to eat

The following is a detailed description of the five categories and some ways in which your kids can earn check marks in each one.

CHORES DAILY

Throw out those complicated chore charts! One blank chart can be used for all behaviors and categories of the CHART method. As the parent, you can add to it as you see fit. Right now, our six-year-old daughter has three daily chores we expect her to do: (1) make her bed and open the window shades in the morning; (2) feed the chickens (we have a small brood of hens); and (3) unload the dishwasher. Any additional chores I want her to do on a particular day fall under the "Acting as asked" category.

Keeping daily chores simple helps your kids stay motivated. Select tasks that are age appropriate, and try not to exceed five daily chores or fewer. This makes daily chores a part of your kids' routine and means your kids will be less likely to put up a fight when you ask them to do them. The completion of each chore is worth one check mark. If your kids don't do their chores, they risk a consequence, such as having their technology time taken away or forfeiting their favorite toy for the rest of the day.

Keep the list of daily chores consistent for a while, so your kids get the hang of doing the same thing every day. A daily routine instills a rhythm that your children will adapt as they grow into adulthood.

Early on, don't expect your kids to do their chores without a reminder from you. My daughter has been making her bed by herself for over a year, but I still have to ask most mornings whether she got it done. Some days, she remembers on her own and makes the bed; other days, she says she forgot but gladly goes to do it. Either way, the bed gets made, and when that happens, my daughter earns a check mark.

One rule we set up from the start was that any complaining or whining about a particular chore means no check mark is earned. When my kids comply cheerfully, they know they will earn their check mark, and they have the added bonus of not having to listen to any nagging from me. There have been times when my kids have grumbled about a task, thereby forfeiting the check mark they could have earned. It's sad when this happens, because they still have to complete their chore. But if you establish a no-whining policy, and assign consequences for any complaints, it helps minimize these occurrences.

HYGIENE

This category encompasses the basic self-care steps you expect your kids to do on their own, without any need for nagging, including brushing their teeth, putting their dirty clothes in the hamper, and getting themselves dressed. If you tend to fight with your kids over what they choose to wear, then make a decision the night before. You may even choose to lay out their clothes for them, and if they dress themselves in that outfit without argument, they earn a check mark. My four-year-old twins earn this check mark if they get dressed without asking me for help.

The purpose of this system is to motivate kids to desire to do things on their own. Creating independent little humans who make good choices is a goal of the CHART method, and hygiene is a major category where independence becomes important.

ACTING AS ASKED

This category of the CHART method is like gold. It's ideal for moments like the one Sheinelle Jones recently related on the *Today* show. She wanted her daughter to accompany her to a speaking event where she would be addressing a group of kids, and her daughter was fighting her on it. Sheinelle promised her daughter a trip to the store to purchase any toy she wanted, if she would simply come along, behave well, and be a good listener. If Sheinelle had been using the CHART method, she could have offered her daughter one or two check marks for doing what was asked of her. It is amazing how motivated kids become to do what's asked of them if the eventual reward is something they really want.

If the reward is too meager, the system won't work. That's why it is important for parents to figure out what their child wants most (within reason and in accordance with their budget). Is it a trip to the water park? Is it a mom-and-son day out? Is it that toy he's been eyeing? Is it a deposit in his piggy bank? Figure it out when you're making the chart and write it at the top, so your child knows what he is working toward from the get-go.

Our daughter recently earned a pink kayak for our camping trips. The kayak cost $99 and took her months to earn. She hadn't earned it by our first camping trip this season, but that's okay. Not having it yet made her even more motivated to earn it before the following trip. Every day she would ask my husband and me what she could do around the house to earn extra check marks. The CHART method allowed us to create an environment where our daughter wanted to work hard to earn something she wanted.

"Acting as asked" check marks can be particularly helpful in public settings. In that moment when you're shopping and your child is crying for something they want you to buy, tell her that if she calms down by the time you've counted aloud, slowly, from ten to one, she will earn a check mark. You are rewarding good behavior, in the form of emotional self-control—a parenting win.

"Acting as asked" also covers all those tasks around the house for which you want willing helpers. For example, when the playroom gets especially messy, I let the kids know that we are going to clean it together; cheerful and hardworking helpers will earn a check mark. Those who aren't helpful or eager will not earn a check mark. The goal is to motivate good behavior and a healthy work ethic—two invaluable traits that will propel your kids to success in the real world. Using the CHART method to motivate good behavior and a positive attitude benefit children for a lifetime.

READING

Reading is vital to child development. Readers become leaders! Teaching your kids the habit of reading daily is important, and the CHART system can help.

Our daughter has been able to read on her own since completing kindergarten. She earns a check mark for every book she reads out loud. This gives her ample motivation to fulfill our goal for her to read three books each day.

For younger children who cannot yet read on their own, you can use daily family reading time as a way for them to earn a check mark. If they are good listeners who sit still for the duration of a story (or a series of stories), they earn a check mark. If this setup sounds too "easy," you can integrate reading comprehension into the process of earning check marks. After you read a book to your children, ask them some questions about it. Have a conversation about the plot, the characters, the theme, and so forth. In doing this, you improve their reading comprehension skills. Give them a check mark for participation.

TIME TO EAT

Last summer, our daughter was diagnosed with a pediatric eating disorder called ARFID (Avoidant/Resistant Food Intake Disorder). She participated in a program at the hospital that made use of a chart system with check marks to motivate young children to eat. The program worked well with our daughter, so we incorporated an eating category into the CHART method. It can work for any child—even the pickiest of eaters. We use this category with our twins, as well, catering it to their specific dietary needs.

For example, if we are serving a vegetable with dinner that our twins are not overly fond of, we reward them with a check mark if they eat a certain amount of the vegetable—usually half the portion. When it comes to our daughter, she must eat her entire main course in order to earn a check mark. She also earns a check mark for drinking the healthy smoothie I make for her each night. She has thirteen minutes to drink the smoothie. If she does so without complaint during the allotted time, she earns that check mark for the evening.

This system can help you to make sure your kids get the necessary nutritional intake. If your children struggle to eat their vegetables, then start offering them the chance to earn a check mark by eating a specific portion of their vegetables at dinner. Start with small steps to help your children get the "win." You can increase the amount you require your kids to eat over time. For the twins, we began with asking them to eat three bites of the food in question in order to earn a check mark. After several weeks of their successfully finishing three bites of a specific food, we upped the required amount to half a portion. The CHART method can be a way of encouraging children to try new foods and come to enjoy them over time.

SOME TIPS FOR USING THE CHART METHOD

MONEY AS A REWARD

As your children get the hang of the CHART system and begin to understand the value of money, you can assign a monetary value to a completed chart. Our six-year-old daughter earns $20 for each 50-box chart she completes. Right now, she is working toward earning a $99 toy she wants. You get to determine the value of your child's check mark sheet. I recommend starting lower, because you can always increase the amount later on. Lowering the amount after the first chart is completed can be disheartening to your child, so I wouldn't set the bar too high or too low. Again, the reward does not have to be a set dollar amount. Your child could be working toward earning a family game night, a trip to an amusement park, a bowling outing, a specific toy, or a special night out with a parent. Whatever you determine is fair and will motivate your child to earn check marks is wisest.

TAKING AWAY CHECK MARKS

We try not to take away check marks from our kids' charts. Our preference is to motivate good behavior with the promise of check marks. If they misbehave or disobey, we make use of time-outs and the taking away of favorite toys and electronics. The threat of a lost check mark, while it can effectively discourage poor behavior, can also make kids question the point in even trying to earn check marks. For that reason, I keep the removal of check marks in my back pocket, using it only if absolutely necessary. For example, our twins were acting especially wayward at their swimming lessons recently. They had already lost their tablet privileges for that day. The moment I threatened to take away two check marks if they didn't listen to their swim instructor and finish the lesson, they perked up and listened. They obeyed their instructor and finished the lesson. It was the threat of giving up what they had worked so hard to earn that made them obey.

Save the threat of lost check marks for when it is truly needed—those emergency situations when all else has failed.

KEEPING TRACK AND MAINTAINING MOTIVATION

If you can't keep track of which children are assigned which chores, the chart provides a space for writing out such specifics. You can write next to each letter what is expected of each child. For example, our daughter has a different set of chores from our sons. The kids also have different reading requirements for earning a check mark in that category. All these details can be written at the bottom of the chart under the corresponding category.

Be sure to fill out the line at the top of the chart (or paste a picture there of the reward, if your kids aren't readers yet). The system won't work unless your kids are aware of what it is they are working toward. Make sure it is something they are willing to work for, or the system will fail.

When you start using the CHART method, be enthusiastic and maintain a positive attitude that will get your kids excited. You want the process of starting the CHART method to be a fun experience for your kids from the very start. Cheer your kids on, and praise them when they earn a check mark. Once they have been following the CHART method for a while and have earned a reward or two, they will become more self-motivated, which means it will take less effort on your part to get them to earn their check marks.

You can find printable versions of these charts free of charge on my website, Living Joy Daily: www.livingjoydaily.com. Just type "chart method" in the website's search bar.

HIRING HELP

Now that you have some ideas for getting your kids on board with helping out around the house, thereby lightening your load, it's time to look at the jobs that remain on your plate. Do you still feel overwhelmed by everything you're expected to do? Then it's time to take an objective

30 Check Marks to Earn:_____

1	2	3	4	5	6	7	8	9	10
11	12	13	14	15	16	17	18	19	20
21	22	23	24	25	26	27	28	29	30

CHART Method
Chores daily
Hygiene
Acting as asked
Reading
Time to eat

www.LivingJoyDaily.com

50 Check Marks to Earn:_____

1	2	3	4	5	6	7	8	9	10
11	12	13	14	15	16	17	18	19	20
21	22	23	24	25	26	27	28	29	30
31	32	33	34	35	36	37	38	39	40
41	42	43	44	45	46	47	48	49	50

look at your finances and see what jobs you can afford to hire someone else to perform. Every household is different, so be realistic about your own situation. It may be that you aren't in a position to hire a professional maid service. If that is the case, make sure your kids understand the nature of your situation, so they understand just how essential it is that they help around the house.

If you are in a position to hire some outside help, then do your research and find someone who comes highly recommended and whose services you can afford. We have a cleaning crew that comes to our house twice a month. It would be great if they came on a weekly basis, but something else in our budget would have to give in order to make that possible. A bimonthly professional clean is fine by me, and I am happy to clean on the weeks they aren't scheduled to come. The kids are required to help me with these in-between cleans, and they also join me for a full house pickup before the cleaners come. They understand that we pay the cleaners to spend a specific amount of time cleaning our house, and if we want them to focus on the tough stuff—scrubbing the bathrooms, vacuuming the hard-to-reach places, and so forth—then we need to have the house picked up ahead of the cleaners' arrival. If the house isn't picked up when the cleaners come, then the hours we pay them for "cleaning services" will likely be used up just clearing the floors of our messes.

When it comes to delegating, I always say you should hire someone to do the work that you like the least. For example, scrubbing toilets (self-explanatory) and mowing the lawn (it aggravates my allergies) are at the top of the list of things I prefer not to have to do. We have landscapers who do our mowing, but I still tend our flower beds and gardens because I enjoy that particular aspect of yard work. The jobs that we have elected to delegate are those tasks that we can afford to hire out and are the ones we least like to do.

If your home is in need of some major decluttering and you just don't know where to start, you might consider hiring a professional organizer. A good place to look for someone you can afford is on Facebook or your local neighborhood webpage. Many people offer unsolicited recommendations when they are pleased with a professional service, and most are happy to share a recommendation if you ask for it.

Delegating is easier when you have a problem that requires specialized help beyond your realm of expertise. But when an issue arises that you are capable of fixing, you may need to weigh whether fixing it yourself is worth it. We faced this type of decision recently when all the commodes in our ten-year-old home suddenly lost most of their flushing power. After consulting with our usual plumber, we paid him to snake all the toilets, after which he told us our problem was solved. It was not solved, and we were back to plunging toilets the very next day. I needed to find a plumber who could get to the bottom of our problem, so I posted a request for recommendations to a local moms' Facebook group. In the dozens of replies my post received, one company's name came up multiple times, and a friend of mine attested to this plumber's problem-solving abilities. One phone call and a few hours later, the plumber had diagnosed our problem: the toilet bleach tabs we'd been using had caused the working parts of our commodes to disintegrate. His recommendation was to replace all the toilets. *All five* of them.

I told him I would talk with my husband about it.

My husband is handy and certainly capable of replacing a toilet. The question we needed to ask ourselves was whether it would be worth his time and effort to replace *all five* toilets in our home, or whether it would be better to pay someone to do that job. It didn't take us long to decide. We hired our new plumber to do the work. Once we'd ordered the toilets and they'd been delivered, a few days later, he returned to install them. It was a good job to delegate. Having five new toilets installed wasn't cheap, but it would not have been worth having my husband sacrifice his limited free time to do the job. His time is better spent doing the job he is paid to do so that we can afford to hire plumbers and other professional service providers.

You must weigh the job that you are looking to delegate with the cost that you will incur. As a writer and conference speaker, I am often asked to provide the name and contact information of my personal assistant to individuals hoping to book an appearance or schedule an interview. It almost makes me laugh. *Almost.* I work hard and put in a lot of hours, but the money I earn does not permit me to employ an assistant. It may be that things will change and it will make sense for me to set aside a percentage of my income to pay another person's wages. For now, though, I have made the choice not to hire a personal assistant because the cost would be too high. Meanwhile, the cleaning crew that comes bimonthly to our home saves me between twelve and fifteen hours every month. Therefore, the money we spend on cleaning is well worth it because of the time that it allows me to devote to writing, speaking at conferences, and so forth.

DELEGATE SPECIFIC JOBS TO SPECIFIC FAMILY MEMBERS

I have found that delegating specific jobs to specific members of a family makes it easier to enforce the completion of chores. Some families use a system of rotating assignments, but these can lead to battles over who did something last, or who did it better, or who hasn't done it enough lately. Assigning household duties to specific people helps to limit this bickering about work. It also prevents the confusion that can be caused by continually having to make a new schedule. For more than two years now, it has been my daughter's exclusive job to unload the dishwasher, while her brothers have consistently been tasked with setting the table for meals and taking out the trash. These roles may shift someday—perhaps my daughter will be put in charge of making and packing lunches, and I will have one of her brothers take over the unloading of the dishwasher. Regardless, I have found that when individuals are assigned exclusive tasks, they take ownership of their work, while I'm off the hook for remembering whose turn it is to do something. When the dishwasher has finished its cycle, I simply say, "Brielle, it's time to unload the dishwasher."

When I was growing up, I hated doing yard work. The worst possible thing anyone could have asked me to do would have been to mow the lawn. That doesn't mean I never did it. My parents made us kids rotate jobs. I understand their approach—they wanted each of us to learn how to do all the different jobs around the house, and they also wanted to divide the work equally. However, I would have rather done ten loads of laundry and cleaned the entire house top to bottom than mow the lawn once. I told them as much. Eventually, they realized they could actually ask me to do more indoor work, and I would willingly—and almost happily—do it as long as I didn't have to mow the lawn.

I still feel that way, and I know now why I disliked it so much as a kid: it made me feel awful. I would be itchy and sneezing for hours afterward. Back then, allergies weren't really considered as a potential ailment. I didn't know anyone with allergies, so I never suspected that allergies were what I was dealing with. Today, I know that even kneeling in the grass will cause my legs to break out in a rash. I avoid mowing like the plague and will never mow my lawn again, if I can avoid it, because of how severely it triggers my allergies.

Your children may not have an allergy that keeps them from doing a certain job, but they may dislike certain household tasks and have a preference or willingness to do others. You won't figure out their preferences until you've had them try out all the possible chores. That's one reason why it's helpful to have your kids perform a variety of tasks when they are young—so they can find their strengths and figure out their aversions. However, when it comes to saving time and streamlining the housework, assigning specific chores is the way to go.

We started with assigning our children very basic chores—two to three a day—when they were six years old. Until that point, they participated in any household work I asked them to do that was age appropriate. The CHART method made it easy for me to ask them to do chores so they could earn check marks.

Now that my kids are all over six years of age, I assign specific daily chores for which our kids earn check marks on their charts. It is so easy when I don't have to rotate jobs or try to recall who did what chore last. Knowing that Brielle is always in charge of unloading the dishwasher means that when the wash cycle is finished, Brielle knows what is expected of her. She doesn't have reason to question my request or to whine and say, "But I did it last time!" That debate is done away with when unloading the dishwasher is her job alone. The same goes for the trash: Charlie is in charge of taking out the garbage cans, while Alex is in charge of the recycling. Those are their jobs.

When you are assigning jobs to various members of your household, be sure to consider the amount of time that it takes, on average, to do each job, so that you can try to portion out the jobs equally in terms of the demands on each person's time. You should also keep age differences and capabilities in mind, making sure the assigned jobs are age appropriate. If you need help coming up with a chore chart, try Google—there are countless examples out there that you can cater to your own family's needs and abilities.

There are additional benefits to delegating specific chores to specific people rather than asking for help on an "as needed" basis. For one thing, you know you have someone on board to complete a task when the time is right—say, when the dryer buzzer sounds or the dishwasher finishes its cycle. It also means that there are clear expectations set for each member of the household. Once someone finishes his or her assigned chores, it's time to relax and enjoy some free time. It's no fun living in a house where you are being asked or told to do things 24-7, as that kind of environment can cause people to feel overworked and powerless to change the situation. All members of a household need to feel entitled to some free time and rest after their work is done. Giving them specific jobs empowers them to do their work while looking forward to relaxing and pursuing their own activities afterward.

 ASSIGNING CHORES IS A WAY OF EMPOWERING YOUR FAMILY MEMBERS TO DO THEIR WORK WHILE THEY LOOK FORWARD TO RELAXING AND PURSUING THEIR OWN ACTIVITIES AFTERWARD.

Delegating specific chores to specific people gives the household a sense of teamwork because everyone has an assigned job to do. It means that managing the household is not up to the parents alone, and the parents don't have to ask for help every time something needs to be done around the house. In our home, if the dishwasher needs to be unloaded, Brielle either notices on her own and takes care of it, or I tell her the dishes are clean, and she goes ahead and unloads them. There is no arguing. There is no debating. It's her job to do, and she is a part of the household team. When we all fulfill our designated roles and get the job done, everybody wins!

DIVIDING WORK BETWEEN SPOUSES

The topic of how to divide the housework between two spouses is more difficult than the question of how to get kids to help with the chores. That is because no household is ever split exactly 50/50 when it comes to how much housework each spouse does. Every household is unique. If you are unhappy with the division of labor in your home, then you should talk to your spouse about it, making sure you take certain factors into consideration. For instance, are you a stay-at-home mom married to a husband who works fifty to sixty hours a week? If so, is it really reasonable to expect him to do exactly half the housework? Probably not. You should consider each spouse's workload outside the home before deciding what jobs he or she should be responsible for at home.

I work from home, while my husband works outside the home in a job that requires a great deal of travel. He does not have any specific assigned jobs in the home because of the amount of time he spends out of town. It would be ridiculous for me to count on him to complete any regularly scheduled chores. There are certain jobs that he sometimes takes on when he is home, such as cooking dinner, but I never expect him to do these jobs. We might discuss our meal plans for a given week that he's in town, and if I'm approaching a writing deadline, I may ask him to be in charge of dinner for a few nights. Of course, this doesn't mean he has to cook the meal; he can always order takeout or pick up a premade meal. But on evenings when he is out of town or has conference calls that run late into the evening, it would be unrealistic for me to demand that he take care of dinner as part of his "job." His job is being the main financial provider in our home. That's the way our family is structured. Your household may be completely different. I am simply offering my personal story as an example.

A good time to talk about household duties and your expectations of who should do what within the home is actually before marriage, when you are dating. You may have missed the boat on that already. If you are not happy with the situation, then have a conversation with your spouse. Make sure it's a *conversation*, not a confrontation. Try to see the situation from your spouse's point of view, and then seek to help your spouse to understand your own point of view. Talk about the specific aspects of the workload and identify the areas in which you would most appreciate additional help. Again, be sure to take into consideration the other person's workload outside the home, as well as any other pressures. If your spouse is like my husband, he or she may be gone Monday through Friday some weeks; asking him or her to do chores all weekend will make life pretty miserable. Nobody wants to come home on the weekends only to do more work.

Everyone is entitled to some downtime and relaxation. If you are feeling overworked and without any downtime, even on the weekends, then it's time to look at the possibility of hiring outside help if your spouse is unable to fill in the gaps. Bringing in a house cleaner once or twice a month, hiring a neighborhood teen to mow the lawn, or calling in a babysitter or a mother's helper to give you a break so you can get some work done—all these are options that may be worth considering if your workload is beyond your abilities and your spouse is unable (or unwilling) to help. Talk it out and set reasonable expectations for your spouse and for yourself. Approach the conversation with empathy and a desire for both of you to enjoy downtime together on a regular basis. That should be the overall goal: getting your work done so you can enjoy your free time together.

For some couples, this will be such a sore subject that they would be wise to consult a family counselor or a therapist who can help both spouses to talk through the problem and find a solution that works for everyone involved.

CHAPTER 6:

ROUTINES ARE A MUST

Routines can help a household run far more efficiently than it otherwise would, so that a family can function at its best. You may not even think your family has a routine, but you probably do. Routines comprise the activities that you do on a consistent basis—many of them daily— that become habitual. In our home, for example, getting the kids off to school in the morning is a process that usually follows the same routine. We eat breakfast, and then everyone gets dressed, brushes teeth, and combs hair before gathering backpacks and belongings and heading out the door for the day.

If you haven't yet adopted the method I suggested earlier of having a home for every one of your belongings, then it may be that you search for your keys, or your kids search for their shoes, every day before leaving the house—even those activities are part of your routine (an unnecessary part, I might add). Minimizing or even eliminating certain activities in our routines can help us better manage our time. We need to pay attention to the routines we have established, either intentionally or by accident, and see if there are any negative, time-draining behaviors that are slowing us down or preventing us from keeping an optimal schedule.

THE BENEFITS OF NIGHT-BEFORE PREPARATIONS

Having outfits and backpacks ready the night before any school day or workday is a good habit. Growing up, I was required to lay out, the night before, everything I would need the following day, and our household follows the same policy. At night, before going to bed, my three sisters and I had to drape the outfits we had chosen for the next day over the hallway railing, with our backpacks beneath them on the floor so that we weren't searching for them in the morning when it was time to go. We were permitted to change our minds and pick different clothes in the morning, but only if we had enough time and if we also returned our original outfit to the closet. School lunches were made the night before, as well.

During the week, I choose the outfits my kids wear to school each day, including underwear and socks. They wear these clothes without complaint—even my eight-year-old daughter—because this is a routine we have agreed on. Eventually, my daughter will prefer picking out her own clothes and laying them out the night before school. For now, though, she seems to enjoy how I select her outfits and coordinating accessories, such as headbands, bracelets, and necklaces. This routine ensures that even the sleepiest, hardest-to-wake kids have a fair shot at making it out the door fully clothed and on time. We keep the kids' backpacks and shoes by the door to eliminate frenzied searches for those items on school days.

Anything that can be done the night before should be done the night before. This kind of advance preparation is a priceless gift you give yourself. When you wake up in the morning knowing that everything you need for getting out the door is in place, it offers you a running start. It even makes it easier to get out of bed! Starting your day becomes more enjoyable when you have done as much prep work as possible the night before. If you go to bed without making preparations for the following day, the list of what needs to get done in the time before you head out the door can be daunting—lunches to make, outfits to iron, homework to finish, and so forth. Nothing is worse than starting out the day feeling overwhelmed! It's far less jarring to hear that morning alarm go off when you know that your outfit is ready and waiting for you, your kids have their own clothes laid out for them, all their homework is done, and their backpacks are ready and waiting by the front door.

If you begin each day with thoughts of the long list of things to get done within your first waking hours, then you need to rethink your morning and evening routines. Evening routines should be used to help you start your next day right. Waking up knowing that you prepared the night before is like arriving to an exam having studied and prepared the day before; waking up without having prepared the night before can feel like waking to a pop quiz or a final exam without any preparation. Do yourself a favor and prepare the night before. Here are some things that you can incorporate into your nightly routine that can help you get a jump start on your mornings:

+ **Review your calendar and consider what you have going on the next day.** Taking this step will help you mentally prepare for tomorrow. It can also help remind you of things you should take care of sooner than later. For instance, you may read on your calendar that you have a morning meeting to attend, and you signed up to bring muffins. Rather than having to rush out the door the next day so you have time to stop and purchase muffins on the way to the meeting, you might purchase them the day before, or even bake them yourself. Having the time to plan gives you more options. It also makes you less stressed the next morning.

+ **Go over your to-do list.** Check off what you accomplished today, and anticipate what needs to be done tomorrow. (We will talk in greater depth about to-do lists in a later chapter.)

+ **Create a time-block sheet.** This is a method of writing down a schedule for yourself that builds in your activities as well as your downtime. (We will cover this idea more toward the end of this chapter.)

+ **Lay out your clothes for the next day.** If you plan to go to the gym after work, pack a bag with any clothes and accessories you will need for the gym, so you won't have to go home to change. It saves time when you have everything ready to go and you don't have to return home for changes of clothes or shoes.

+ **Prepare your breakfast.** If you prefer to eat a little later in the morning, you may choose to take your meal to go, packing it in a lunchbox. This makes it easy to grab and go, and it will discourage you from stopping for fast food if you get off to a late start.

+ **Pack your lunch.** If you take your lunch to the office or wherever you go, prepare it beforehand, pack it in your lunch bag, and stash it in the refrigerator the night before. In the morning, just grab it and go!

*   **Have a to-go pile.** Put your to-go items by the door, on the kitchen counter, or someplace else that works consistently for you. I like to lay out my personal items on the kitchen counter the night before—usually workout clothes in a duffel bag, a pair of flat shoes in a carryall bag (if I start the day in high heels but plan on running errands later), and any materials I need for meetings throughout the day in a laptop bag. Preparing these items in a consistent location means I can take everything with me in the morning without having to stop back at home throughout the day.

SETTING ROUTINES FOR KIDS

Kids thrive on routines. Consistency in as many areas as possible can help them function well. If your children know that they are to get up in the morning by six thirty, with the expectation that, in the hour between six thirty and seven thirty, they are to eat breakfast, get dressed, brush their teeth, and do anything else required to prepare themselves for school, then they are more likely to get on board. On the other hand, if they are permitted to sleep until a quarter past seven—or if they get up on time, only to lounge around until you shout a ten-minute warning—it's likely to be a panicked rush getting them out the door. Having a consistent morning routine keeps you and your kids from starting the day feeling frazzled. In this way, a daily schedule is just as important as a schedule of chores—it keeps life running smoothly and also teaches your kids to become responsible. It helps them become planners who establish the healthy habit of doing things in a timely manner so that they don't end up late for school, extracurricular activities, social events—and, eventually, work.

Getting kids on board with a morning routine involves outlining your expectations of what time they should get up and also what time they should go to bed. Be sure to enforce these times to ensure that your children get enough sleep. Children who haven't gotten enough quality sleep will be difficult to wake for school in the morning. If you have trouble getting your children out of bed most school mornings, then you may need to reassess their bedtime.

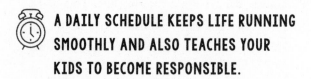 **A DAILY SCHEDULE KEEPS LIFE RUNNING SMOOTHLY AND ALSO TEACHES YOUR KIDS TO BECOME RESPONSIBLE.**

Holding your children to a morning routine helps them to become responsible individuals who can get themselves ready in the morning and arrive on time to their daily activities. An after-school routine is just as important. This does not mean that you should schedule every minute of their day. Children need periods of freedom within healthy boundaries. It isn't unreasonable to institute the rule that your children must complete their homework before going outside to play with their friends. If they choose to go out and play before their homework is done, you should take away a privilege, such as screen time. You should also tell them a specific time when they are to come home. Don't keep reminding them with text messages; set a time beforehand, and if they are late due to reasons within their control, impose a consequence. This teaches them responsibility.

You don't need to be a helicopter parent, but you should strive to help your children understand the importance and usefulness of sticking to a schedule and following the rules while they live under your roof. Freedom within boundaries is the key. Parents must set appropriate boundaries and rules, so that their kids have the freedom to develop responsibility and learn firsthand the personal benefits of routines.

When you give your children freedom *and* expectations within reasonable boundaries, you are teaching them to develop responsibility for their behaviors. For example, if you assign them chores that they must complete each day, and you set the time at which they have to go to bed, then they can figure out how much time they have to complete their chores between waking and bedtime—and it's up to them to get them done. As a consequence for the failure to complete their chores, you might withhold their allowance or temporarily take away a certain privilege.

The most effective consequence I've found for motivating my own children is the removal of their tablet time. Every day, my kids are given a set amount of time to play games on their tablets. If they forfeit that time because they've broken a rule, then they know it was their own actions that lost them that privilege. You aren't being a "mean parent" if you follow through with a consequence you established ahead of time. You can empathize with them and say, "I am so sorry I have to take away your tablet time for tomorrow. I wish that you would have done your chores tonight so you wouldn't have lost this privilege."

ROUTINES CREATE CALMNESS

Households that run on routines tend to be calmer homes than those that don't. When children don't know what to expect at home and cannot anticipate what is coming next, it can cause them stress and anxiety. This is the reason many preschools and daycares post their daily routines, using a series of pictures, on the classroom wall. Schedules help to set routines, which create a calm, predictable environment in which children can thrive.

It's this predictability, brought about by schedules and routines, that makes for a calmer household. When a household lacks a morning routine, and the times for waking up and getting ready vary greatly from one day to the next, there is bound to be a lot of rushing around on the mornings when everyone wakes later. This rushing around causes stress and anxiety. It is not a good way for anyone to start the day. We can help our kids—and ourselves—start the day right by setting a specific time to get up on school days and detailing a specific process for getting ready. Establishing a set time by which everyone is to be ready makes that routine come together and gives everyone an understanding of how long they have to get ready each morning.

Imagine hearing your spouse say to you, "We need to leave right now!" when you thought you had thirty minutes more to get ready. How would it feel, having to pull yourself together and get ready at warp speed in order to leave on time? Can you imagine the level of stress and frustration you might feel? This is exactly how your children feel when they don't know what time they are expected to be ready in the morning, and you are barking impatiently at them to get going.

If the time you decide to leave the house varies from one morning to the next, your children may never really know, on any given morning, what time they need to be ready to go. This type of uncertainty can cause them stress and anxiety. Most young kids don't have the emotional intelligence to ask their parents to set a specific departure time in advance. As a result, their morning routine becomes fraught with stress and turmoil as they try to guess when you will tell them it's time to leave.

In our household, the goal is to leave the house by seven twenty on school days. My twins are still learning to tell time, so they depend on me to say, "Ten minutes left," "Five minutes left," and then "Gather up your things and get in the car!" My giving them several warnings like these helps them stay on track with the morning routine, so that they aren't just half dressed and stressed out when it's time to leave. My daughter is old enough to watch the clock for herself. She has become accustomed to managing her time in the morning because of our set schedule and the morning routines we have established.

Our kids learn their habits from us, their parents. If we often sleep late and spend our mornings rushing around trying to find our keys, purse, or wallet, our children are likely to pick up those same behaviors. But if they see us holding ourselves to a schedule and moving with purpose every morning—and if we expect the same of them—then they will be more likely to get with the program. We should set a good example by establishing consistent morning routines that allow us to get ourselves ready at a pace that is manageable yet calm, not terribly rushed or stressed. Moving with purpose is a good habit. However, moving fast because you are habitually running late, resulting in stress, is not a helpful habit to pass on to your kids—nor does it make for a pleasant parent!

ROUTINES OFFER STABILITY

When a shelter-in place order was put in place for our county because of the COVID-19 pandemic in the spring of 2020, our family needed to establish a new routine. For one thing, school was going to be conducted at home, meaning we would have to come up with a daily schedule. The schedule we created helped to define a new sense of normal in our home. It provided stability in the form of a guide for how our family would conduct ourselves going forward. Just because we were staying home didn't mean that bedtimes were abolished or that schoolwork could get done whenever the kids felt like doing it. We set a schedule to establish a new routine so that we weren't feeling stress and anxiety because of a lack of structure.

When your life is turned upside down, one of the best things to do is to continue established routines as closely as possible—or to establish a new routine you can follow. An utter lack of routine—days upon days of unpredictability—compounds any stress we may be feeling. Kids may grow anxious if they have to wonder who will make their dinner and when. They are bound to feel stressed if they don't know whether they are supposed to be doing schoolwork or whether they can go outside and play without getting in trouble. The unknown is scary for children, just as it can be for adults. We can help our kids by setting specific times for specific activities. This way, they can know what they are supposed to be doing at any given time during the day. When kids know what they are expected to do, and when, it prevents their days from being a stressful guessing game.

 WHEN KIDS KNOW WHAT THEY ARE EXPECTED TO DO, AND WHEN, IT PREVENTS THEIR DAYS FROM BEING A STRESSFUL GUESSING GAME.

How is your household routine? Are there segments of the day that your children would consider a guessing game? Do they know what is expected of them throughout the day, and is there a routine that enables them to anticipate what comes next? If not, it's time to consider setting up a daily routine.

SETTING UP A ROUTINE USING BLOCK SCHEDULES

Before you start setting up a routine, whether it's for yourself, for your kids, or for your entire family, you first must recognize the *needs* versus the *wants* in your schedule. Needs are the things that *must* take place as part of your daily schedule, such as meals, wakeup time, and bedtime. The musts can help build the main structure of your schedule. Work times and school times are also a part of your daily routine.

Once I have identified the essential tasks for the day, I like to break my day into chunks of time, thereby creating a block schedule that helps me know what I need to be doing throughout the day in order to complete my to-do list while still making it to any prearranged appointments and getting my work done. The following is a sample block schedule of a typical weekday for our family, when school is in session. I have broken my day into chunks of time and specified what must get done during each of those chunks.

- 6:30–7:20 a.m.   Kids and I get ready for the day.

- 7:20–7:40 a.m.   School drop-off (play family devotional in the car on the way to school).

- 8:15–9:15 a.m.   Workout at barre studio. (Bring outfit to change into so I can go directly to Bible study from the studio.)

- 10:00–11:30 a.m.   Bible study.

- 12:00–2:30 p.m.   Go home, eat lunch, and work on writing or conference presentations. Return two phone calls from to-do list.

- 2:30–3:15 p.m.   School pick-up; listen to my book in the car.

- 3:15–5:30 p.m.   Help kids with homework; make dinner; clean up kitchen after dinner; have kids get ready for lacrosse practice.

- 5:30–6:00 p.m.   Drive to lacrosse practice.

- 6:00–7:00 p.m.   Lacrosse practice. Bring along work to do while watching practice from the sidelines.

- 7:00–7:30 p.m.   Drive home.

+ 7:30–8:00 p.m.   Bedtime routine for the kids.

+ 8:00–9:00 p.m.   Prep for the next day; do final house pickup.

+ 9:00–10:30 p.m.   Personal downtime—reading, catching up on social media, and/or watching TV.

As you can see, my schedule is built around daily appointments—school pick-up and drop-off—and any work that I need to get done. Having my routine set and written down the night before helps my next day run as smoothly as possible, because I have mentally prepared myself for what needs to get done and the time frame involved. For example, seeing that I plan to work out and then go to Bible study, and that I want to change clothes at the studio in between these two events, let me know that I should lay out two outfits for the day. The workout outfit will be laid out in my bathroom, to be put on in the morning, and the outfit I'll wear after working out will be put in a duffel bag and laid on the kitchen counter for me to grab on my way out the door in the morning.

If you are new to the process of setting up a routine using time blocking, grab a notepad, a pen, and your calendar. Record any appointments you may have the following day. Then, factor in other essential places and times, such as being at home when your kids get off the school bus or making dinner. Break up your day into corresponding blocks of time.

Be realistic about how long it takes you to get where you're going so that you give yourself enough time to reach your destinations in case there is traffic. The average drive time to my kids' school is twelve minutes, but on days with heavy traffic, it can take as much as twenty minutes. Therefore, I always put twenty minutes on the schedule. If I end up with some extra time between school drop-off and my barre class, I may make a phone call that was on my to-do list, or maybe I return some emails. Obviously, I don't catch up on correspondence while driving. Any extra time while I'm behind the wheel is spent listening to audiobooks. I have been an avid audiobook listener for years. This practice helps to keep me focused on the road and prevents me from even glancing at my phone. I tend to have one fiction and one nonfiction book downloaded at any given time, so I can pick which of the two I want to listen to while driving in the car. It's when I have parked—having arrived early for an exercise class or to pick up my kids from school—that I catch up on emails or phone calls.

Consider your longer periods of free time and any extra time between appointments and must-do activities. How do you plan to spend that free time? Try using it to accomplish items on your to-do list. Rather than procrastinating until the last minute—for instance, trying to purchase Valentine's Day cards the day before they are due to your child's school (they'll be hard to find, believe me)—put the item on your to-do list immediately after you become aware of it. Then, when you find yourself with an open block of time, you can tackle these to-do list items. You will be doing your future self a favor by working ahead and getting things done in advance. If there is something I know will need to be done, whether sooner or later, I add it to my list and aim to accomplish it as early as possible. This is how I stay on top of my to-do list.

It is up to you how much you put on your to-do list, how far in advance you put it there, and how far in advance you want to work on each item. When should you begin your Christmas shopping? To answer that question, you need to figure out when you would like to have your shopping completed so that you can enjoy the Christmas season. I like to start my Christmas shopping in October and finish it by Thanksgiving. Our family does our Christmas decorating by the Thanksgiving deadline. That way, I can relax during the month of December, knowing that I am prepared and can sit back and enjoy any holiday events with my family.

Deadlines of this nature are subject to personal preference. Figure out what it will take for you to enjoy a particular season, and then put deadlines in place to ensure that you have freed up enough time to spend the holidays doing the things you enjoy. If you are rushing around putting up decorations and doing all the family shopping the two weeks before Christmas, then you may be having to turn down party invitations, and you will feel stressed by the looming deadline of the 25th.

Planning your daily schedule in such a way that allows you to complete items on your to-do list, even months in advance, will help you feel empowered. You are taking control of your time and your future when you complete tasks well before their deadline. Only you can make it happen for yourself, though, and it comes down to the daily decisions you make regarding how you spend those blocks of extra time between scheduled "must-do" activities. If you waste that time surfing social media or watching TV, that is your decision. Yes, we all need downtime, but how much downtime is really needed each day? How much of that daily downtime would be better spent tackling items on your to-do list?

Decide for yourself how you will spend your day tomorrow, and block out your time now. If you make up your mind to work on items from your to-do list, then you are more likely to follow through. If you leave it up to what you feel like doing in the moment, you will likely fall back to whatever is easiest and has been your fallback habit, such as scrolling emails and social media on your phone. Set yourself up for better time management tomorrow by deciding today how you want to spend each block of time, along with the tasks you believe you can complete from your to-do list during any downtime or open blocks. Organizing your day the night before is one of the most helpful things you can do to have a productive tomorrow. When you set up time blocking with specific tasks you want to accomplish, you are giving yourself intention and purpose for the day ahead.

CHAPTER 7:

WORK AS THOUGH EVERYTHING WERE URGENT

It is remarkable how fast we can get the house cleaned when we find out that someone is going to be stopping by in half an hour. A home can go from a complete wreck to being picked up, wiped down, cleaned, and company-ready in almost no time at all when we have a pressing reason to get the job done. If you're looking for motivation to complete your housework, I recommend pretending you're expecting company, or otherwise putting yourself in "panic mode." A sense of urgency, even if it is self-generated, can transform the way you complete your tasks and run your household.

This chapter and the tips it conveys may be the key you need to unlock your productivity. I didn't start off the book with this chapter because it is important to master much of the previous content before you follow the tips shared here. If, for example, you have not shaken the tendency toward perfectionism, the techniques in this chapter won't work for you. I may set a goal for myself to fold a single load of laundry in five minutes' time. Sticking to this speed should allow me to fold four loads of laundry in twenty minutes. However, if I am a perfectionist who insists that the underwear be folded a certain way (in truth, I don't fold my underwear or the kids' underwear; those garments go straight into the underwear drawers unfolded), or if I make a habit of refolding certain items until I'm satisfied with the result, then it will slow me down. I need to set aside the determination to fold everything "perfectly." The goal is to get the job done and to keep moving forward. Get it folded, put it away, and move on to the other things you need to do, and you will eventually enjoy some downtime.

SETTING TIME LIMITS

For most household tasks, I set a time limit on my completion of them. This helps me to get jobs done. They may not be done to the utmost perfection, but they get done. When I set myself a time limit, I move at a faster pace and complete the job in the least amount of time possible. It is important, however, to be realistic when establishing time limits for different tasks. The following are some of the limits I've set for myself for specific household chores:

+ Making my bed, opening the window shades, and picking up the bedroom: 15 minutes

+ Cleaning up the kitchen after dinner: 30 minutes

+ Clearing my car of any debris left behind at the end of the week: 10 minutes

+ Cleaning the chicken coop: 30 minutes

+ Vacuuming the main areas of the house: 20 minutes

+ Weeding the front lawn: 2 hours (shh…I like to do this task at a leisurely pace so I can listen to my Audible books and enjoy the outdoors). This is a good time for me to point out that there may be tasks that you should do at a leisurely pace because you enjoy the process. Many of my friends prefer working at an unhurried pace in the kitchen because they relish such tasks as cooking and baking. Allow yourself the freedom of taking as much time as you can afford for the tasks that you enjoy.

+ Performing final pickup around the house before going to bed: 20 to 30 minutes

+ Folding a basket of laundry: 5 minutes. (It is important to know how many loads of laundry your own washer holds. We recently replaced our old washer and dryer with machines that are nearly commercial size, so they hold four standard loads each. This means that if I fill them to capacity, a single load is four loads in one; thus, it should take me twenty minutes to fold a load that has been filled to my dryer's capacity.)

+ Washing the kitchen floor by hand: 30 minutes

+ Vacuuming the upstairs: 20 minutes

✦   Sorting the playroom with the kids' help to get things back in order: 1 hour (We try to do this "playroom refresh" at least once every other week. Even when the kids have been picking up after themselves and putting their toys away on a daily basis, some items end up in the wrong bins or mixed with other toys. A biweekly reorganization gives us an opportunity to put things back where they belong.)

These are just a few examples to get you started thinking about the amount of time you might allot for various household tasks. These times are flexible, of course—they're a general standard I use that can be changed as needed. If the kids and I go to sort the playroom and find it particularly messy, I may allot us an hour and a half to clean up and sort everything. You can create your own chart of routine chores and set yourself specific time limits for completing those chores.

PUT IT INTO PRACTICE

The next time you find yourself with a long list of items to do around the house, try to put some time limits into practice. Let's say that, tonight, I need to clean the kitchen, vacuum the main floor, and fold and put away four loads of laundry before doing my final bedtime pickup. I know that the kitchen is a thirty-minute job, vacuuming the floors in the main area of the house should take twenty minutes, folding four baskets of laundry requires twenty minutes, and picking up the house before bedtime will take twenty minutes. This means that if I work at a good pace, I can get all this work done in an hour and a half. Therefore, as I start tackling these projects, I will keep an eye on the clock and set my pace according to the time periods I have allotted myself for each job. This tactic will keep me from getting distracted by checking my phone or being pulled to other tasks, because I am motivated to get a specific job done in a specific amount of time.

How many of us can admit that there are times when a job that should take only thirty minutes, such as cleaning up the kitchen after dinner, turns into a two-hour chore? We may check our phones or get distracted by our kids, a TV show, or an email message that we opt to respond to immediately. The job that should have taken only half an hour of focused worktime drags on and on, because we keep getting distracted and having to restart the task. When we stick to a task, pushing distractions aside, we keep our momentum going and are likelier to complete the job in one fell swoop. But if we decide to respond to that email, then, for example, the countertops that we already washed may be left to air dry, resulting in spots and streaks. After we send the email, we realize we forgot to dry the counters, and we have to start over, washing the countertops once more and then drying them this time. We compound our work, costing ourselves additional time to complete a job because we stopped mid-process. Multitasking can seem like a great idea, but it can also slow us down. Starting and stopping during a job may cause it to take us far longer than usual to complete.

 WHEN WE STICK TO A TASK, PUSHING DISTRACTIONS ASIDE, WE KEEP OUR MOMENTUM GOING AND ARE LIKELIER TO COMPLETE THE JOB IN ONE FELL SWOOP.

I encourage you to take on just one job at a time and finish it before moving on to something else. The only way that I have found multitasking feasible is when I listen to Audible books or podcasts while I work. This habit usually motivates me to do work because it is only when tackling tasks that I allow myself to listen. But multitasking in the form of doing three different jobs at once is not often fruitful in the long run. It divides your attention and causes the work to take more time overall.

When you focus on one job, you save time by not having to redo any of the work, and you can maintain a momentum that helps you finish faster.

WRITE IT DOWN

When I first began the practice of timing my household tasks, I would write down what I did and how long it took me. Using the example above, my written record might look something like this:

+ 6:00–6:30 p.m.   Clean kitchen

+ 6:30–6:50 p.m.   Vacuum main area of house

+ 6:50–6:10 p.m.   Fold four baskets of laundry

+ 6:10–6:30 p.m.   Pick up the remainder of the house

Then I would watch the clock as I got started with intention and purpose. My goal would be to finish each job on or before the next time slot began. A written schedule would help me to focus on what needed to be done during each specific period of time. I would not switch back and forth between jobs, nor would I pause to check social media or reply to emails. Allowing myself to get distracted would just about guarantee that my whole schedule would be thrown off, and I would end up working far later into the evening than I would like. Following a strict time frame, on the other hand, means I can look forward to the reward of downtime when the jobs are done.

Even if I fall a little behind because a particular job takes me longer than I expected it to, I don't get upset or frazzled. I can shift the time slots of the remaining tasks on my schedule accordingly. The goal is getting things done with intention, purpose, and momentum. Even if those things take slightly longer than anticipated, I can guarantee that you will accomplish them more efficiently with a time schedule than without one. If you were to tackle those tasks on a given night without a schedule, you could easily spend twice as much time doing them. Why? Because you would be more willing to allow interruptions, and your attention would be more easily distracted by social media, TV, or something else. Setting a schedule with an allotted time frame for each job establishes an expectation for yourself regarding how long you want each job to take you.

Interestingly, I have noticed an occasional discrepancy in the time it takes me to clean the kitchen: some nights, I get the job done in half an hour, while on other nights, it may take me a full hour. How is it that the same amount of work can sometimes take me twice as long to complete as usual? It happens when I fail to maintain my usual pace. We must consider each job and allot ourselves the amount of time that it ought to require us to get it done. If we can achieve the same results by working just a half hour as we would have by working a full hour, then we should allow ourselves a half hour for that task going forward. Working at a pace that's slower than your optimal ability is a time killer. In order to be productive and efficient, we must work at a pace that maximizes the time we spend on it. But when we allow ourselves too much time to complete a task, we tend to slow down and fill that space with our less-than-optimum efforts. Set for yourself time allowances that are realistic, yet require you to move at a steady momentum to get the job done.

The same goes for your kids. If you give them an hour to get a job done, they will probably fill that entire hour by pacing themselves accordingly. But if you were to tell them to do that same job in half an hour or forty-five minutes, they could probably finish it in that time span, especially if given enough incentive. And the ability to do what they want after they finish the job should be incentive enough!

MAKE USE OF INCENTIVES

I set time limits for myself on my evening tasks because, if I didn't, I would be working until midnight—and even then, the work would not be truly done. Our work is never "done," so the important thing is to accomplish what is most pressing while putting off the rest until those items become more urgent. Looking around my house at any given moment, I might notice walls that need washing, rugs that need cleaning, and furniture that could use some touching up. However, if I can't go to bed at night until my entire house is in perfect condition, I will get hardly any sleep! It would require my staying up until at least two or three in the morning to keep my home super clean all the time—definitely not worth it.

Everyone needs downtime—a chance to relax and unwind. The activities that constitute downtime will differ from person to person. Many of us unwind by binge-watching our favorite TV shows. Others may unwind by catching up on social media. Figure out what best helps you unwind, and use that activity as extra motivation to get your work done in the allotted time.

One of my Netflix series is releasing the first episode of its third season tonight. I look forward to watching the show, but I have a few items on my evening to-do list that I need to accomplish first. For one thing, I need to finish writing this chapter. I am giving myself an hour to do this. Second, I need to clean up the kitchen, which will take about thirty minutes. Third will be my nightly pickup around the house. It is now six in the evening. If I stick to the schedule I've set for myself, I can be watching my Netflix show by eight o'clock—perfect timing, since the kids go to bed between seven thirty and eight. Knowing that this time of unwinding and relaxing with Netflix is ahead of me, I can stay on task and resist the temptation to check my phone.

Phones can be our biggest distraction. They keep a lot of work from getting done. Check your average phone usage, and you may be shocked to discover how many hours you spend on this device on a daily basis. Put the phone down, possibly after turning off any unnecessary notifications, and get working. Push through the desire to pick up the phone every few minutes. You can catch up on everything after your work is done.

Two hours from now, I will do just that—catch up on emails and check social media while watching a Netflix show. Staying on task is key to increasing productivity and saving time. Start making the conscious choice to avoid picking up your phone when you are working toward the completion of a specific list of timed tasks.

While I am cleaning the kitchen and doing the final pickup around the house, my husband will be helping the kids through their bedtime routine. How did we come up with this particular division of labor? I gave him his options and let him pick what he wanted to do: either clean the kitchen and do the final house pickup, or put the kids to bed (not always an easy feat, as most parents have probably realized). I didn't have a preference, but I figured he would probably opt to put the kids to bed, since he doesn't prefer doing the final pickup of the house. I don't mind. My two tasks take about an hour combined. His single task will also take about an hour, between making sure the kids have bathed and brushed teeth, reading them some stories, praying with them, and tucking them in for bed. We divide and conquer.

When it comes to delegating household tasks to my husband, I always try to defer to his preferences. This is because I keep in mind that our family depends on his income, not mine, and thus his schedule should be the priority. If he has a series of conference calls planned throughout the evening, it means I do all the evening tasks—including putting the kids to bed—myself. My husband's job requires flexible hours and frequent late-night, early-morning, and even middle-of-the-night phone calls because of varying time zones. He does what he can around the house and with the kids when he is off work. I also understand that, just as I do, he needs regular downtime. Our marriage is a partnership where we both try to do our best and help as much as we can. We aren't perfect, but what matters is that we always try to consider and appreciate the workload of the other person, and to pitch in accordingly.

Using incentives such as downtime is helpful not only for ourselves, but also for our kids. If I assign my kids a chore, I often tie it to a time limit and an associated reward. For example, if my kids want to play on their tablets in the morning before school (which they do, every day), they know that they must first get dressed, eat breakfast, and brush their teeth and hair. If they should happen to sleep late, leaving themselves little to no time to get ready, they don't get to use their tablets that morning. But if they wake up early enough and get ready ahead of time, they can enjoy half an hour or so on their tablets before we leave for school or begin our homeschooling for the day. Whether or not they get morning tablet time is up to them. This policy is a simple way of teaching them to budget their time wisely.

If my kids get on their tablets before they have gotten ready for school, there are consequences. I don't tell them the consequences after they have broken the rule—that wouldn't be fair. Rather, when we instituted the rule about morning use of tablets, I informed the kids that if they got on their tablets before they were completely ready, they would lose the privilege of using their tablet for the entire day. Setting up these rules and then following through with them by enforcing the prearranged consequences has been a great way of teaching my kids time management as well as responsibility.

You must figure out which incentives work for your kids. Maybe your children don't play on tablets, but they love their LEGOs, or they are fond of a particular show. Figure out a way to use these pastimes as incentives—and to come up with related consequences. Be reasonable, though. If you find yourself taking away their privilege almost every day, you may need to objectively assess your expectations of them. Some kids require more prompting to get ready in the morning. It may begin with your waking them up, then setting a timer for them to get dressed. If needed, set a timer for them to eat breakfast, too, as long as this method doesn't make them feel too rushed or frazzled to eat. (Instead of a timer, you could play a favorite song whose duration is the amount of time you want to allow.) If our children get ready on time, they get to enjoy the predetermined privilege or incentive.

You may need to work with your kids for several weeks, spurring them on and helping them get ready in the allotted time, before you require them to get ready all on their own. This process will help them develop the habit of getting themselves ready at a decent pace—a skill that will help you in the long run, because who wants to have to start the day shouting at their crabby, slow-moving teenagers to get ready? Set your children up for success as teens and young adults by helping them develop efficient preparedness methods now.

MAXIMIZING RESULTS WHEN GETTING READY

My kids have their own incentive to get ready in the morning— being able to play on their tablets before school. My personal incentive is to look decent when I leave the house. I like my sleep, so I am not about to get up an extra hour early just to have time to get myself ready. I prefer getting as much sleep as I can and using shortcuts that enable me to be ready in fifteen minutes' time. Yes, you read that correctly—fifteen minutes in the morning is all I need. People who see me out during the day would probably never guess that it took me a mere quarter of an hour to get ready. The reason is that I make use of the following time-saving methods—methods that can save you time, too, and still help you to look your best.

MOVE SOME PREPARATIONS TO THE NIGHT BEFORE

I know I've discussed this habit several times already, but I cannot emphasize its importance enough! Get as much stuff done the night before as you can. Two preparations that I do in the evening that save me considerable time, energy, and decision-making effort in the morning are showering and laying out my clothes, along with the shoes I plan to wear and any accessories I want to pair with the ensemble.

USE ACCESSORIES TO YOUR ADVANTAGE

It's the finishing touches—jewelry, accessories, hairstyles, and the like—that make you look polished, as if you took a long time to get ready in the morning, and probably earn you more compliments than anything else. Jewelry and accessories are easy enough to select ahead of time, when you are picking out your outfit the night before. When it comes to hair, I don't have time to style mine every day. I do my hair and wear it down without any accessories about two days a week. The other days, I wear a headband, put on a hat, or pull my hair up in a bun.

I love hats. I wear all kinds of them. In the summer, I wear wide-brimmed hats and sun hats that match my sundresses. In the winter, I wear berets, cloches, and hats that could be described as 1920s Gatsby style. Many people have said to me, "I wish I could wear hats; I just don't look good in them." The key is finding a shape and style that complement your face. Not all hats look good on me. In fact, cowboy hats make me look dreadful. I live in Texas, and I haven't yet found a cowboy hat that looks good on me! The style simply doesn't work with my face shape. If you're interested in making hats a part of your wardrobe, you should try on a wide variety of styles and sizes; eventually, you're bound to find a hat that works for you.

In my case, I have found that the wider the brim, the better the hat looks on me. That may not be the case for you. Maybe a more petite brim would suit you better. No one can say that all hats look terrible on them unless they have tried on every style. I can almost guarantee there is at least one hat style that would complement your face shape and enhance your appearance. Once you have found a hat you like, you can purchase that style in various colors and fabrics to coordinate with your wardrobe.

Wearing a hat that complements your outfit can give the impression that you put a great deal of effort into getting ready, when, in reality, you may have cut corners because you didn't have time to style your hair. When you have greasy, stringy hair that would take you at least twenty minutes to fix with dry shampoo and a full hour if you were to wash it in the shower, then blow-dry and straighten it, why not give yourself an easy out? Hats will become your new best friend when you find two or three that go with your basic everyday style.

Other days of the week, when I am not wearing a hat or doing my hair, I wear a headband or put my hair up in a bun. When I use a headband, I may have to use some dry shampoo first and then put my hair in a ponytail—a process that takes all of five to seven minutes. Headbands are another accessory that you can add to your ensemble to make it look as if you tried harder than you actually did. I usually lay out a headband or a hat that coordinates with the outfit I've selected the night before I plan to wear it. Sometimes I lay out both accessories, thereby giving myself two options in the morning. If the headband isn't cutting it and my hair is in worse condition than I thought when I went to bed, I opt for the hat.

I have purchased enough headbands to go with virtually every outfit in my closet, and they weren't expensive, either! The overall cost was certainly less than a single trip to a salon (a place I never visit, since I dye my own hair and do my own nails—details forthcoming). All I can say is, I'm glad headbands are in style once again! I searched Amazon for knot headbands and found thousands of options, including many sets of ten or twenty at a bargain price. Having a wide assortment of colors allows me to match any given outfit with a headband, freeing up a lot of time I might have spent styling my hair in more complicated manners. By itself, a ponytail looks pretty plain and doesn't give the impression that you took much time to do your hair. But a ponytail paired with a headband makes you look more polished and put together, especially when the headband goes with your outfit and you wear additional accessories, such as a necklace and earrings.

Of course, you need to do you. If you aren't a headband person, then don't feel that you need to start wearing headbands. I am simply recommending something that has worked for me and gotten me countless compliments.

The third hairstyling option that I like to use, besides hats and headbands, is the bun. I use a "bun maker," of which there are many different styles; mine is textured in such a way that it grabs my hair. It's shaped like a long sphere with two ends that snap together, making it a cinch to turn a simple ponytail into a polished, professional-looking hairdo—one that conceals the bun maker in its entirety and makes it seem as if I'm a highly skilled hairstylist. This five-minute method is the way I usually style my hair when I speak at conferences. Now you know my secret to having hair that appears professionally styled in five minutes flat!

COORDINATE YOUR ACCESSORIES

I make accessorizing easy on myself by purchasing coordinating sets of earrings and necklaces and by storing these matching items together. If I were to separate the earrings from their coordinating necklace, I would probably spend several minutes searching for one part of the set I had selected to wear on a given day. That time adds up. Four minutes each day, times seven days a week, is twenty-eight minutes. That is almost half an hour a week spent locating sets of jewelry that match your outfits.

Maybe you don't wear jewelry, perhaps because it takes too much time to pick out. Think about reorganizing your jewelry and storing coordinating sets together so you can easily find them and lay them out, at night, along with the outfit you plan to wear the next day.

DRESS UP (AND STOP THINKING IT TAKES TOO MUCH TIME OR ISN'T COMFORTABLE)

Another trick I use to look more put together, without actually doing anything extra, is dressing up. If you know me, you know I "dress up" almost every day. (I don't consider my outfits to qualify as "dressing up," but most other people would.) I don't go out in public wearing yoga pants unless I am actually coming from a workout class. On most days, I wear dresses and leggings.

You may be thinking, *Dresses? Comfortable? Are you kidding?* If that's the case, allow me to respectfully disagree. Just hear me out: the dresses I like to wear are comfortable, first and foremost. I won't wear anything that is overly constricting. My dresses (which are often mistaken as tunics, since they are on the shorter side and paired with leggings) are more functional than they look. Just because something is dressy-looking doesn't mean it can't be comfortable. Made from the right material, a dress can be just as comfortable as jeans and a T-shirt—maybe even more comfortable. As a matter of fact, I rarely wear jeans. I find denim to be uncomfortable, constricting, and completely unforgiving of even the tiniest amount of weight gain. Meanwhile, if I wear my stretchy dresses, my weight can fluctuate without any discomfort because my clothes fit regardless. Leggings, too, I find far more comfortable than jeans. Pairing leggings with a dressy tunic or a dress makes me look like I put far more effort into getting ready than I really did.

I have a question for you. Is it any more difficult to put on a dress and leggings than a T-shirt and jeans? Don't these outfits require the same amount of time to put on? Of course, they do! Why other people seem to think I put more effort into getting myself ready than they themselves did is a mystery to me.

For a week, or even for just a few days, try laying out dressier outfits than you would normally wear. Make sure that the fabric is stretchy enough to be comfortable. If they are tight-fitting tops that offer little to no freedom of movement, you are likely to give up on the experiment. Choose fabrics that feel nice on your skin. Dressing up doesn't need to be uncomfortable.

Once you've laid out your "dressy" outfit, select coordinating jewelry and a headband or hat. Be sure to pick out a pair of shoes that goes with the outfit, too. Here in Texas, we wear boots half the year. I like boots made of suede or faux suede that have a little heel. It is amazing how even the slightest height of heels can take an outfit from average to wow. Try it out: put on an outfit with flats first, then try it with heels of any height and note the difference. You may not be the heel-wearing type of person, or maybe you can't bear the thought of going an entire day in heels because of the amount of standing and walking you tend to do. Pick your footwear based on your level of activity, keeping in mind that you can always bring a backup pair of shoes. Even on days when I wear heels, I often put a pair of flats in the car in my carryall bag, for changing into if I decide, after any formal meetings or appointments, to run errands at Walmart or Target. Of course, I lay out both pairs of shoes the night before, and I start the day in whatever pair makes sense, taking the other along in my bag. This pattern of preparation saves me the time it would take to run back home between appointments for a more comfortable pair of shoes (and it saves me the discomfort of toughing out a shopping trip in stilettos). Save yourself time—and save your feet—by laying out two options for footwear the night before and planning to take both with you the next day.

BUDGETING TIME IN THE WORKPLACE

I use time allotments for more than just housework—I also use them on the job, as I prepare for the various conferences where I am a featured speaker. Whether it's planning a presentation, organizing the materials I'm going to share, rehearsing what I will say, or loading up my vehicle and traveling to a conference, I apply my time-budgeting method. Why wouldn't I? Deciding what to pack for a conference and then loading my vehicle could easily take four hours or more. But by referring to a laminated list I make, in advance, of what I need for each conference, I can load my vehicle in about an hour. This list ensures that I don't forget anything. Setting a specific time allotment for the task also helps me focus on what needs to be done without getting sidetracked or distracted.

 SETTING A SPECIFIC TIME ALLOTMENT FOR A TASK HELPS YOU FOCUS ON WHAT NEEDS TO BE DONE WITHOUT GETTING SIDETRACKED OR DISTRACTED.

You should objectively look at your workload and see where you can implement time budgeting. I can tell you that this method of budgeting time truly propelled me into my writing career. When I started blogging, I had very limited time to write. My daughter was four, and the twins were toddlers—a handful, as you can imagine! I decided that I would take only one hour to write each blog post. This determination helped me to focus on what I really wanted to say and to get the writing done quickly. After drafting a post, I would proof my work only once. Believe me, I received plenty of emails from readers pointing out my various typos and other mistakes. However, I decided it was more important that I do my blogging in the allotted time frame than to worry too much about any mistakes. I realized that if I were to wait to publish my blog posts until they were absolutely perfect, then my blog would be pretty bare—as would my professional portfolio.

It was the self-taught ability to get my posts written, proof them quickly, and get them published that made writing feasible for me. I know many writers who will author an article and then proof it twenty to thirty times before they publish it. This process may work for them. For me, however, I would rather produce, quickly, a higher volume of articles, hoping at least a percentage of them would resonate with my readers, than spend thirty hours on an article that might end up being a dud.

My advice is that you decide how much time it takes you to do a job effectively, without having to make it *perfect*. Take that time that you decide is appropriate, and apply it to your workload. You will likely find that you become a producer when you apply time allotments and stick to them. Find a time frame that allows you to do great work—without your going into the crazy zone of nitpicking and insisting on perfection. Set time limits that allow you to do quality work. If you are a blogger, maybe you need two to three hours to write a post you can be proud of. Don't compare yourself to me. Each of us is unique. Use your best judgment on your own workload and how long it should take you to complete a task. Set for yourself time limits that allow for quality work and then stick to those allotments of time. You will soon find yourself becoming more productive and efficient.

CHAPTER 8:

TAKE A BREAK FROM GOURMET MEALS

If you can't already tell, I like shortcuts. This is especially true when it comes to cooking. There was a time when I enjoyed spending time in the kitchen preparing gourmet meals at a leisurely pace. When my husband and I were first dating, and even early on in our marriage, we spent a great deal of time cooking together. Now, however, our home can be very hectic with three children, a dog, a flock of chickens, and both of us working. We need to exercise discernment about how we spend our time. It was nice cooking together for hours in the kitchen every evening all those years ago, but there is no way we have that luxury now, with other humans and living beings demanding our time and attention. Although gourmet meals made from scratch may have taken a backseat for the time being, it doesn't mean we can't enjoy delicious, healthful meals on a regular basis.

Just because we don't have a lot of time for cooking nowadays doesn't mean we order from restaurants on a regular basis. We want to raise our kids to appreciate healthy food and well-balanced meals. They learn from our habits, so we try to introduce a wide variety of healthy food options at dinnertime that we all eat together. A dinner that comes together quickly is not necessarily unhealthy.

SUGGESTED SHORTCUTS FOR HEALTHY, TASTEFUL MEALS

The following are some of my favorite shortcuts to make healthy meals at home using minimal effort and time.

PREMADE MEALS

This is my favorite of all shortcuts. I like to purchase meals that are fully prepped and simply require baking at home. The stores where I like to shop, such as Costco and Sam's Club, have premade family-sized meals in their refrigerated area. These meals come packaged in disposable aluminum containers, and the instructions are simple: remove the plastic lid and bake according to the instructions. Some of our family favorites the past few years from these locations have included meat loaf with mashed potatoes, chicken fettuccine alfredo, chicken pot pie, and fully loaded flatbread pizza. The options that these stores provide make it easy for me to purchase an assortment of meals, and I typically pick as many as three or four on a weekly basis. Baking them at home means we enjoy them fresh from the oven, but someone else did all the prep work. Buying premade meals saves me hours of time each week.

I have also broken down the price on what it would cost for me to buy the ingredients myself versus the costs of these premade meals. With the two particular stores where I like to shop for groceries—Costco and Sam's Club—it is actually just as cost effective, if not more so, for me to buy the premade meals instead of making the same dishes from scratch. Therefore, not only am I saving time buying these premade meals, I am also saving money.

Many grocery stores also sell premade meal options in their deli and fresh-food sections. These can also be a good time-saving option, though they may cost you more on average than similar meals at budget stores such as Costco and Sam's Club. You can find options; you just have to do some research at your grocery stores.

MICROWAVE-STEAMED VEGETABLES AND SALAD KITS

Another favorite shortcut of mine is using steamers or steamed vegetables in a bag. These products can be found in the frozen-food section of your grocery store. The packaging makes it possible for you to microwave the vegetables directly in the bag, which means you can have freshly steamed vegetables ready in ten minutes or less. There is a wide variety of brands that offer this option, meaning the prices are usually quite reasonable.

Our family also enjoys bagged salad kits that include lettuce and other greens, dressing, and toppings such as shredded cheese, sliced nuts, toasted sunflower seeds, croutons, and so forth. Some of our favorite types of these salads are described by the manufacturers as dried strawberry salad, Asian salad, and chopped Southwest salad. Mix it all together, and you have a fresh-made side dish, or a main dish that you can top with some grilled chicken or another meat, ready in under five minutes.

Bagged salad is a go-to of mine when we are entertaining guests. Especially in the summer, when we tend to host many pool parties, my husband will grill up some meat, and I will put together the side dishes—usually including one or two salads from a kit, which allow me to spend minimal time in the kitchen so I can keep an eye on my own kids in the pool rather than assign lifeguarding duties to my friends for too long. Having friends over doesn't mean that I'm required to make everything from scratch. Providing nutritious food that tastes good is what really matters. And I will say that even most kids seem to enjoy my salads made from a kit!

 IT ISN'T TOILING FOR HOURS OVER GOURMET MEALS BUT PROVIDING NUTRITIOUS FOOD THAT TASTES GOOD THAT REALLY MATTERS.

MICROWAVABLE RICE POUCHES

There are many companies now making rice and other grains easy to cook at home in less than two minutes. In the aisle of your grocery store where you would look for big bags of rice, you will find smaller pouches of rice that are microwavable and ready-to-eat in minutes. Even though these pouches are smaller than the bags of dried rice, a single package is usually enough to serve as a side dish for our family of five. We may need to prepare a greater amount when my kids get older and are eating more. For now, one package is all we need. If we have company over, I increase the number of rice pouches accordingly. These rice pouches are the quickest, easiest way I have found to cook rice. They come in a variety of flavors and types of rice, too. We like garlic butter, jasmine, and basmati.

BREAD FROM A BREAD MACHINE

I love the smell of freshly made bread in our home. I also love the taste of fresh bread versus almost any kind of bread I can buy in the store. However, I don't want to have to spend a great deal of time making bread. Our family likes using a bread machine. It takes about three hours for the bread to bake, but only approximately ten minutes to combine the ingredients in the machine and press start. I ordered our bread machine online after researching a wide variety of types, focusing on brands that reviewers had described as "beginner friendly" and "easy to use."

When making bread, I follow any one of the recipes printed in the user's manual that came with our machine, or I use a recipe that I found online. Our kids prefer white bread and butter bread. To make the process even easier, I order my flour and yeast on Amazon and have them shipped to our home.

We enjoy fresh homemade bread on a weekly basis thanks to the shortcut of a bread machine. The bread machine does all the real work, mixing and kneading. It also takes care of the rise and bake times. Easy "homemade" bread doesn't have to take hours of your time.

GROCERY PICKUP AND DELIVERY

If they didn't prior to the COVID-19 pandemic, most stores now offer delivery and pickup options, either free of charge or for a small fee. I like Walmart grocery pickup because it is currently free to use. After selecting my groceries on the Walmart app and placing my order, I receive a notification of some options for a one-hour pickup window, usually the next day. I select the time I would prefer, and then, the following day, I drive to the store, park in one of the designated spots for online order pickups, and use the app to let the store know that I'm ready for my order. Then I pop the trunk of my vehicle and wait for someone to load the groceries into my car. Depending on how many customers show up to collect their orders at any given time, I may wait anywhere from ten to twenty minutes from the time I pull into the pickup spot to the time I head home with my order.

Making use of online ordering and grocery pickup has been a tremendous time-saver for me. There are still occasions when I choose to go to the store and do my own shopping so that I can browse my options in person. Most weeks, however, I use my app and place an online order. In years past, I would shop for groceries once or twice a week, with each shopping trip taking me between two and three hours, including my drive time. Now, my weekly time investment in grocery shopping is just thirty to forty minutes, since I place and pick up just one order each week.

I still shop at Costco and Sam's Club, but I typically go to those stores once every other week. Often, our family will shop together at one of those stores on the weekend. That is when I tend to buy a selection of premade meals. Anything that I can't get at one of those two stores, I add to my cart on my Walmart app while I am shopping. That is one feature I appreciate about the Walmart app—being able to add items to my cart and to leave them there until I'm ready to check out. I can add groceries and other items, such as paper towels, toilet paper, and cleaning supplies, throughout the week rather than having to add them all at the same time. This way, instead of keeping a running grocery list that I type out or write down, I simply add the items I need to my cart on the app until I'm ready to pick them up at the store.

Amazon Fresh is another option that we have used for grocery orders, though I tend to prefer Walmart for its lower prices overall. Aldi is another bargain option, though their online ordering requires the use of Instacart, an app that incurs a yearly subscription fee. If your favorite grocery store offers delivery or pickup options, I would highly recommend trying it out. Not only does this service save me significant time, it also saves me money because I purchase only the things I decide I need ahead of time, rather than strolling the aisles of a store and adding all kinds of unnecessary products and impulse purchases to my shopping cart.

I will be sticking with grocery pickup as long as the items available on the app cost the same as they would if purchased in store, and as long as the service is offered for free or at a nominal cost. For me, it's a no-brainer, since it frees up multiple hours in my weekly schedule to be spent on other, more enjoyable activities—maybe meeting a friend for lunch, the expense of which I can justify because of the money I'm not spending on impulse buys at the grocery store.

STORE-BOUGHT COOKIE DOUGH

During the Christmas season, I always make cookies from scratch—it's a yearly tradition our family enjoys. The rest of the year, however, I rarely have enough time to prepare and bake cookies from scratch. So, how to satisfy my kids' love for the smell and the taste of fresh-baked cookies? I purchase readymade cookie dough from the grocery store. There is a wide variety of options available, as far as flavors go, as well as some different styles of dough—most commonly, a carton that you scoop from, a log of dough for slicing and baking, or a scored sheet of dough that you can break apart and place on the cookie sheet.

I prefer the dough that I can scoop from the container and shape myself. I buy chocolate chip cookie dough in a plastic tub that I store in the refrigerator, so I can bake as many cookies at a time as I want to. My kids like to help bake these kinds of cookies, too. It may be a "cheat," because we haven't mixed the ingredients ourselves, but it gives us the pleasure of eating freshly baked cookies—plus, it makes our house smell so good.

FROZEN MEALS

Another option for meals throughout your week is frozen meals that you bake or microwave. We have a deep freezer that makes it easy for me to keep plenty of frozen dinners on hand, so I always have a fall-back plan for nights when I don't have a premade dinner in the fridge or enough time to prepare a meal from scratch.

One of our favorite frozen meal staples is pizza. We have pizzas regularly, even when we are making a conscious effort to "eat healthy"—I may purchase gluten-free pizza, Lean Cuisine pizza, or another weight-conscious brand of pizza. I also keep regular pepperoni pizza on hand, since that is an overall favorite in our household.

Our family also enjoys Chinese food, and there are many frozen meal options in this particular genre. One of our go-to brands is P.F. Chang's. Most of their frozen meals are sold in a bag and require you to simply heat them up in a skillet. I like to pair these dishes with a packet of microwavable rice and some microwave-steamed vegetables for a tasty meal that is on the table in less than twenty minutes.

I also like to purchase frozen lasagnas, boxes of frozen garlic bread, and other premade pasta meals from the grocer's freezer section. These items can take an hour or more to bake, so some advance planning is required, but the actual effort on your part will be no more than a few minutes. Most of them require you to simply remove the meal from the box, place it in the oven, and bake it. The directions are easy to follow; just be sure you allow yourself enough time to be at home to get it baked before dinnertime. A frozen lasagna, paired with garlic bread and a bagged salad, gives you a flavorful dinner that will make your kitchen smell wonderful.

What matters most is not the time that it takes you to cook a meal; it's that your family is being served food that is nutritious and tasty. Fast-food meals may seem like the biggest time-saver, but you can invest just as little time into preparing healthy, balanced, tasty meals at home using the shortcuts I've mentioned. You don't have to cook everything from scratch or do all the meal preparations yourself. Taking advantage of premade meals allows you to cut down on time and save money while still cooking at home.

CHAPTER 9:

IDENTIFY AND ELIMINATE TIME WASTE

Our habits determine how the minutes and hours in our days are spent. It is time to get honest about how you spend *your* time during an average day. Do you tend to just go with the flow, paying little attention to the passage of time, so that whatever is going to get done will get done, and that's that? Or do you move with purpose and intention during your waking hours?

ADDING INTENTION TO YOUR DAYS

Moving without intention and purpose is a major way of wasting time. But you can save yourself time and not waste even a minute when you move through your day with intentionality. If you wake up in the morning knowing what you want to achieve by ten o'clock because you have made a to-do list for the two hours between eight and ten, you are more likely to get those tasks done in a timely manner. But if you wake up without any plans for your day, you are likely to accomplish everything you set out to do—absolutely nothing. You will probably while away your day with no sense of direction or purpose, whether it's scrolling through social media, gaming, napping, or engaging in other unproductive activities.

Your aim should be to move through each day with purpose and direction, at a pace that will allow you to achieve your goals according to the time you've allotted yourself for each task. The way that I keep myself moving purposefully is by using time blocks based on my to-do list. Let's look at an example of how I might spend a morning meeting multiple goals I've set for myself:

- ✦ 6:30–7:20 a.m.   Get myself and the kids ready for the day.

- ✦ 7:20–8:00 a.m.   Drive the kids to school, drop them off, and return home.

- ✦ 9:00–10:30 a.m.   Tackle to-do list items: Place grocery store order for pickup tomorrow; call to make a dental appointment for Charlie; call groomer to schedule an appointment for

Max; fold four baskets of laundry; call
Mom.

+ 10:30–11:00 a.m. Drive to doctor appointment.

+ 11:00 a.m.–noon Doctor appointment; work on responding
to flagged emails while seated in waiting
room.

The example above maps out a single morning, from the moment I
wake up until lunchtime. You can see how I have broken up the time into
blocks, factoring in such details as drive time, in order to have realistic
expectations of how my morning should flow. The block of time from
nine until ten thirty has been set aside for completing specific items
from my to-do list. If I were not to allocate that time specifically for
those tasks, then the probability of my accomplishing all of them would
be low. When we designate a set time period for the accomplishment of
specific tasks, we increase the likelihood of our completing those tasks.
But if we don't set aside a time for tackling specific tasks, who knows
when we will complete our to-do list?

Setting schedule blocks in this manner takes us back to an earlier
strategy of self-motivation: giving ourselves time limits on our tasks.
This motivation begins when we outline our expectations for our day
before that day even starts. Set your agenda for the upcoming day by
doing a time-blocking exercise the night before. I like to do this while
unwinding at the end of the day, usually watching TV. It takes me less
than ten minutes to look at my calendar and jot down my blocks of time
for the following day on a notepad that is small enough to be stashed in
the carryall bag I always keep with me. That way, I can easily check my
to-do list during the day and stay on schedule.

Unless you have a photographic memory, you're probably like me—
relying on written lists and reminders to keep you from forgetting anything. You may think that this strategy seems like too much work, but

it's worth it when I think about the time I would waste on a daily basis because of a lack of objectives (or the inability to recall the objectives I set). Creating a nightly to-do list, and blocking your time into a schedule every day, saves time and increases productivity. If you want to be a doer who finishes each day with a warranted sense of accomplishment, this method of creating a schedule around specific tasks is the best way to make your days more productive, starting tomorrow.

You are likely wasting time during the day trying to remember what you need to do. When it is written down, you don't waste that time. The other benefit of writing it down is that you are making yourself accountable to complete the task. Write down your to-do list along with your schedule, so that you save yourself time from trying to recall what you need to get done.

PUT DOWN THE SMARTPHONE

A default activity for many people—myself included—when they find themselves with some free time is to turn to their phone. These devices, which have done wonders in connecting us and making our lives easier, are also perhaps the biggest waste of our time. Whether it's mindlessly scrolling social media, skimming email messages repeatedly, playing meaningless games, or engaging in such soul-harming habits as looking at pornography or chatting with alluring strangers in chatrooms, smartphones waste a lot of time and ruin a lot of relationships.

 OUR SMARTPHONES—WHICH HAVE DONE WONDERS IN CONNECTING US AND MAKING OUR LIVES EASIER— ARE ALSO PERHAPS THE BIGGEST WASTE OF OUR TIME.

As I've mentioned before, you can check your phone's usage history to see just how much time you've been spending on it—daily, weekly, and monthly. You can also set time limits on your phone for just about everything.

Perhaps you would like to reduce your time on social media to no more than half an hour a day. You can set your phone to enforce this half-hour allotment of time, and you can even assign which platforms of social media you would like the rule to apply to. This method is a great way of seeing whether you've been spending too much time on social media.

AN EXPERIMENT

I challenge you to do an experiment, whether or not you think you've been spending too much time on social media. Decide on what you deem to be an appropriate amount of daily time usage for social media, perhaps half an hour or an hour. (If you decide on four hours, it is probably time to reevaluate your priorities—unless, of course, your job revolves around social media.) Once you decide for yourself what constitutes an appropriate daily total amount of time on social media, go into your phone's settings, click on "time management," select "app limits," and specify the amount of time accordingly. After that, proceed as usual, and see if you aren't surprised by how early in the day your phone lets you know that you have reached the time limit you set for social media. If anything, this experiment will help you become more conscious of the time that you spend on social media. It is your phone and your life, so you can always override your limits. However, you should be honest with yourself about how you are spending your time, and recognize how much of your day you are spending on social media.

SOCIAL MEDIA: EMOTIONAL TIME WASTE?

When you are scrolling social media, do you find yourself getting upset? If so, this emotional response could be happening for a wide variety of reasons. Most people, if they spend enough time on social media on any given day, can make themselves upset. One way that people find themselves in emotional turmoil is by seeing pictures of families that appear "perfect." Even during a global crisis and a complete shutdown of society, we still find those parents who seem to be doing everything to perfection: they plan creative activities for their kids—who, by the way, seem like the happiest kids in the world—and it's been nothing but sunshine and blue skies for the family, all through their COVID-19 lockdown.

The appearance is a lie. Nobody has a perfect life, especially during a time of worldwide crisis. There are many people who elect to post only picture-perfect moments on social media. You would never see anything to indicate that their marriage is on the rocks or that their teenager is starting to rebel. Those types of details aren't fitting for the image they project on social media. Wanting to appear perfect to the world, they post only the best moments.

Most people tend to post primarily positive moments to social media. Nobody wants to air all their dirty laundry for the rest of the world to see and judge. Yet this tendency to post exclusively positive pictures and details can produce a skewed impression that others have a far more idyllic life than we do. If you believe that social media conveys an accurate depiction of everyone's lives, then it will probably seem that everybody is far better off than you! Remember, you're never privy to the whole truth—the marital issues, the behavioral problems their kids are having, their financial woes. Some people will share "real" postings from time to time, but most aren't airing even a small percentage of their problems to the world.

Think about your own postings to social media. What percentage of the good parts of your life have you showed to the world—and what percentage of the bad? Don't allow yourself to entertain the belief that everyone else is leading a better life than you. All of us deal with struggles, even the most accomplished, the wealthiest, and so forth. I am not perfect, and neither is my family, but I don't post our daily issues to social media. I prefer sharing good memories and fun experiences because those are the things I want to remember when I scroll through my own history. If someone's social media posts seem too "perfect," give that person some slack. Sometimes, those who are trying the hardest to convey the image of a perfect family are the ones who are hurting the most. They want to convince the world—and themselves—that everything is okay, so they post images that depict an idyllic life, however inaccurate.

Scroll with caution. Know that you are not alone in your problems. Use social media to keep in touch with friends and family and to stay aware of the good things happening in their lives. If you are going through a particularly challenging season yourself, then you may want to limit your social media use even more, or even suspend your account for a period of time. You can make yourself quite upset when your mind is telling you that everyone else has a better life, and the proof is in front of you on social media. The real problem is that the proof is fake. Most people don't show all the details of their lives—the good, the bad, and the ugly.

Another way that you can upset yourself on social media is by reading too many political posts. This rabbit trail has ruffled me a lot in the past. I may be scrolling social media and will innocently comment on a friend's post that was only slightly political—for example, a post highlighting the importance of protecting trees—only to find myself getting attacked by strangers, all because I accidentally opened a can of worms that I don't have time to deal with. In our humanness, we naturally want to defend ourselves and our positions, and we may get sucked into a back-and-forth discussion that is passionate and emotional on both sides. It is remarkable how much time can fly by when we get into one of these discussions on social media.

We aren't likely to change anyone's political views by what we say on social media, least of all people we don't know. The opinion of a stranger doesn't usually carry much weight when it comes to our opinions, so why would we presume to be able to alter the opinion of someone we've connected with strictly on social media? Don't waste your time by getting drawn into the political debates on social media.

EVALUATE YOUR RELATIONSHIPS

Relationships should be one of the most valuable parts of life. Yet there are people who have a draining effect on our emotions and energy. We need to use discernment in deciding whom we spend our time with, because our time is a fleeting commodity. If someone treats you poorly and produces a negative effect on your emotions and self-esteem, then you should consider significantly limiting the time you spend with this person. If you work with this person, you may not have a choice in the matter if you want to keep your job. However, you get to decide on the people you associate with in your free time.

When I first moved to Texas, I was willing to spend time with *any* mom who had kids my daughter's age. I wasn't picky because I was just getting to know people in the area and looking to make new friends. However, after six months or so, I had established a group of friends whom I knew I could count on to leave me feeling encouraged and uplifted as a mom after we had spent time together. We treated one another with kindness and wanted to build the others up on our journey of motherhood. Finding the right friends was important, but I first had to give lots of different people a chance at friendship to find the ones who were the right fit (for me as well as for them).

Not all friendships are meant to be. There are people I have met since moving to Texas whom I have made a conscious choice not to spend much time with. I have come to realize that I should invest in the friendships that I want to preserve for the long haul. Many friends may come and go, but it is a blessing to have a precious few who hang in there with you for ten years or more. Make sure to invest in your relationships with the people you want to count as friends ten years from now. Yes, people can move away, and fallings-out can happen, but it is still wise to be intentional about the relationships in which you make the biggest investment.

 INVEST IN YOUR RELATIONSHIPS WITH THE PEOPLE YOU WANT TO COUNT AS FRIENDS TEN YEARS FROM NOW.

You don't need hordes of friends to be happy. In fact, you really should be focused on three to five friendships, outside of your family members, that you want to keep long term. Dr. Suzanne Degges-White shared an article in *Psychology Today* highlighting her research on friendships in adulthood.[3] She conducted a study of adults in an effort to figure out the number of close friends that most people need, and have, in their lives. It was reported that, on average, adults between the ages of 30 and 70 have anywhere between three and five close friends. These are the type of friends that you can count on to answer your call at two in the morning in a time of need (whether it's a cry for emotional support or there's

---

3. Dr. Suzanne Degges-White, "How Many Friend Do You Really Need in Adulthood?" *Psychology Today*, 9 August 2019, https://www.psychologytoday.com/us/blog/lifetime-connections/201908/how-many-friends-do-you-really-need-in-adulthood.

an actual crisis). Those three to five friends are the relationships that we adults should invest in, according to Dr. Degges-White.

It is wonderful to have many friends who are acquaintances. However, if you are trying to invest deeply in your friendships with ten different people, you are likely spreading yourself too thin, and your family and household will suffer for it. Decide who you want to build your relationships with, and the rest can remain acquaintances. You can't have deep and meaningful relationships with everyone. Time will simply not allow it. Therefore, choose your closest friends wisely, and invest in those friendships.

If you have people in your life who suck up a great deal of your time and leave you feeling used and depleted, then you should limit your time spent with them. I can recall one friend—more of an acquaintance, really—whose company I enjoyed, but her tendency to start political debates every time we were together grew exhausting. She asked me several times to get together outside of the workout classes where we routinely saw each other. I declined every time because I realized that our friendship was not one that I wanted to build. My time is very limited, as is the time of most busy parents. Time I would have spent with her would have been time away from my family. I didn't see her as a friend that I would grow with, because we differed so much in our views. More important, being around her really got me down. It can be emotionally exhausting to feel that you have to defend your views and listen while your perspective is put down continuously. Anyone who insists on mercilessly questioning your point of view is probably not someone with whom you want to build a deeper, more meaningful relationship. You would only be setting yourself up for future hurts.

I want to be around friends who make me feel good about myself and my views. Spending time with my closest friends leaves me feeling energized, uplifted, and inspired. I love being around them because of how they make me feel and what we can add to one another's lives.

As much as you are able, limit the time that you spend with people who make you feel drained of energy or leave you with a negative after-taste. You may not even be able to pinpoint why you don't like being around someone, but the simple fact that you feel bad after being with that person should be enough for you to consider limiting your time with him or her. You don't have to make everyone happy, and you don't have an obligation to spend time with people outside your family who make you unhappy. Let them go. Sometimes, some serious social distancing is for the best! You don't have to confront these individuals and tell them you don't want to be around them any longer. Frankly, that would just be rude. Simply spend less time with them by busying yourself with other relationships and activities. Eventually, those individuals will move on and find other friends. If it is a close friendship you are giving up, please try to create distance between yourself and the other person in a kind and gracious manner. Filling your time with other activities so that you have a true inability to get together with that person is one way to create the needed distance.

Other people are a huge part of our lives. Make careful choices about the people outside your family with whom you spend time during your week. Your family should be a top priority and should thus get the majority of your time and attention. If you are heading out to be with friends every night of the week, then you may need to reevaluate your priorities. Your family is deserving of your time and energy, and they need you. Don't overschedule yourself with so many activities that you deprive your family members of the gift of your time.

FIGURE OUT WHAT YOU CAN SKIP

In my twenties, I developed a rash on my hands and fingers that just wouldn't go away. I went to see a dermatologist who eventually suggested I stop getting my nails done at a salon to see whether that made a difference. Sure enough, once I had my artificial nails taken off, the rash began to recede. I'm not sure exactly which component of artificial nails I was allergic to, but I do know I decided then and there to do my own nails going forward. My solution for perfect-looking nails at home is glue-on nails. I prefer the Kiss brand of French nails, which is available at Walmart, Target, and most drug stores, because it resists chipping and comes in a "real short" length that keeps them from constantly popping off. I have tried longer glue-on nails, and they pop off with just about any amount of pressure. Using the real-short version limits pressure on the nails, and they typically last me anywhere from seven to ten days. (When we go camping, they last only about two days because I handwash all our dishes, so I turn to Color Street nail polish strips for camping trips.)

Both these products—glue-on nails and nail polish strips—last me far longer without chipping than any salon manicure I've ever had. The application of either one takes me about ten minutes now that I'm accustomed to the techniques. By doing my own nails at home, not only am I protecting my hands from rashes, but I am saving time and money every month. The glue-on nails look like they were done in a salon (now that I'm proficient at the technique, at least). With a little practice, you can have elegant-looking nails at a fraction of the price of salon manicures and without the headache of trying to do your own acrylic nails (believe me, I've tried, and it isn't pretty).

Another self-care routine I reserve for the home is hairstyling. When my twins were babies, I started lightening my own hair because it was easier to stay home with the babies than try to find a babysitter while I spent several hours at the hair salon. I was never overly fond of the salon experience, anyway, and I was happy to find a money-saving method that didn't require me to hire someone to stay with my kids. Once I found an all-natural hair product that worked for me, I started doing the job myself, and I haven't looked back. People are usually surprised to learn that my hair is not professionally styled. The truth is, my hair is already blonde, so the lightening that I do is not a drastic change.

If you are going to try dyeing or highlighting, I would advise consulting with a professional. Hair is too easily damaged and destroyed by amateur attempts at certain techniques, so please don't just jump in and do it unless you have some guidance from a professional.

Please also note that I did not write this section with the intention of criticizing anyone for using the services of a salon. Your salon professionals need your business, so, please, don't stop going to them just because I shared my story. I am merely offering, as an example, some ways I have found to save myself time and money. That doesn't mean that you should necessarily do likewise. It may be that going to the salon is a time of pampering that you value highly. In my case, I never really enjoyed going to a salon to get my nails done or my hair cut and styled. The time commitment became a burden, and I figured out that I enjoyed doing my own hair and nails at home. I merely offer a time-saving technique of my own in the hope of inspiring you to find an area of your own life that you may be able to handle yourself, saving time and money.

I am not telling you to give up your salon visits, or any services that you consider pampering. Women need to find ways to relax and unwind during their downtime. Personally, I would prefer shopping for clothes or reading a book. My preferred forms of relaxing may be completely different from yours. Do what fits for your lifestyle and meets your needs. You don't have to do what I do. I am only trying to help you look at your own life and consider any areas where you can start doing things yourself to save time and money.

OTHER WAYS WE WASTE OUR TIME

There are some other areas where you may be wasting time during your day without even realizing it. Below are some behaviors that waste time that you may notice in your own way of living. Recognizing these habits and behaviors is the first step toward change.

NOT WORKING DURING THE WAIT

When you go to an appointment (dental, chiropractic, and the like) or find yourself waiting in a line (for example, at the DMV), how do you spend your time while you wait? Do you get any work done, or do you spend the entire time surfing social media? If we don't have a plan for how we will spend our wait time, we will typically *waste* that time. Have a plan for what you want to get done while waiting for an appointment, so you can take advantage of that time rather than letting it go to waste.

COMPLAINING

Complaining never solved anything. Not only does it waste your time, it also wastes time for whoever may be listening. It is okay to problem-solve and vent about an issue where you are legitimately seeking a solution. But complaining just for the sake of whining is not a good use of time.

DOING WORK THAT OTHERS ARE SUPPOSED TO DO

If you are doing work for others that they should be doing, stop. Let other people do their own work so you can use your time to do what you need to do. The tendency to do others' work comes up a lot among parents doing their children's chores. If you have assigned a job to your children, don't do it for them. "Helping" them in this way isn't doing them any favors; you are only conditioning them to take you for granted. Instead, teach them responsibility by expecting them to do their own work—and enforcing the consequences if they don't.

INDECISION

Indecisiveness has wasted many people countless hours. In general, you should strive to use whatever information you may have to make a decision and move forward. For example, don't be one of those people who, at restaurants, can never decide what they want to order from the menu. You drive everyone around you crazy by taking twenty minutes to order. Make up your mind and stick with it!

FOLLOWING CELEBRITIES

Celebrity watching can be entertaining. I personally like to check in on the lives of the royal family from time to time. However, we shouldn't make it a daily habit. Too much time focused on the lives of people we will probably never meet is a waste of our time.

TELEVISION

Watching television can eat away a significant amount of time without our realizing it. When you turn on the TV, pay attention to your start time, and set a timer if needed. Is it okay to binge-watch during your downtime every now and then? Of course. We've all probably done it. However, we shouldn't shirk our responsibilities by spending too much time watching television. Plus, a late-night binge-watching session may rob us of energy for the tasks we need to tackle tomorrow.

TRAFFIC

Traffic can suck up our time, especially during rush hour. Try to get your errands and appointments done outside of rush-hour times, if possible. And, should you find yourself stuck in traffic, try to make the best use of the time by listening to an audiobook. If you are a businessperson, you might use times in traffic to listen to books written by the top leaders in your field. You may learn something new, find some entertainment, and discover ways to advance your career, all while you are driving to or from work.

OVERCOMMITTING

It's good to volunteer for worthy causes and to commit time and resources toward helping others. But it's also important not to spread yourself too thin. Learn to say no! If you say yes to everything, you are going to be overcommitted and overwhelmed. Decide which activities take priority in your life (for help, refer to my earlier discussion of your personal/family mission statement). If the activity doesn't align with your life goals, then don't do it. Just say no (politely, of course!).

TEXTING WHEN A PHONE CALL WOULD BE MORE APPROPRIATE

There have probably been times when you have been texting back and forth with someone with such detailed messages that you thought, *We should have just talked on the phone.* If your text is going to take you ten minutes to type, then you can probably say what you want to say more quickly with a phone call. Don't be afraid to pick up the phone and call people. In this text-driven world, we sometimes forget that we can still call one another. If your texting is getting to be too time-consuming, just call the person and talk it through.

DIVING INTO AN ONLINE RABBIT HOLE

Have you ever gone online to research something, only to find yourself clicking on link after link to articles and pages that grab your interest? The clicking can be an endless rabbit hole. Maybe you started out looking up some symptoms that you are experiencing, and you end up on a page where you're reading about what happened to child celebrities from the 1980s. It's called clickbait advertising. The idea is to get you to click on something other than what you are reading, which leads to further clicking and an increasingly distant departure from your initial search. Be cognizant of how your time online is spent. Don't fall for the clickbait and endless Internet rabbit holes.

LOOKING FOR LOST ITEMS

Having to search for an item in our home is a waste of time. This is why, as we discussed in chapter 3, everything in a household needs a place, or a "home." If we are searching for our keys, our kids' shoes, or our purses and backpacks on a regular basis, we are wasting time unnecessarily. Putting things back where they belong is essential to saving time daily.

SEARCHING YOUR EMAIL INBOX

Searching for an email that you need to refer to is a waste of time. By creating a special folder for items that you want to return to—messages you want to respond to, offers you intend to take advantage of—you will make it far easier for yourself to find those emails. I like to flag any emails that I know I will need to reply to within the week. That way, I can easily find them in the flagged folder. Save emails that you think you will need in the near future, and keep them in the appropriately labeled folders so that you can find them without any trouble.

TRYING TO REMEMBER WHAT YOU WERE SUPPOSED TO DO

When we fail to write down what we wanted to get done, we will search our minds, our email inboxes, random pieces of paper we find lying around—anything, really—in an effort to figure out what it was that we intended to do. Written or typed to-do lists and shopping lists can save you a great deal of time and brain-wracking. You know what you are supposed to do when you write it down. Writing things down can be one of the biggest time-savers that helps you accomplish your intended tasks more efficiently, as we will discuss in greater depth in the next chapter.

CHAPTER 10:

MAKE USE OF CALENDARS AND TO-DO LISTS

Calendars and to-do lists are crucial for anyone who wants to be a productive task manager who gets things done. It is difficult to make it to your scheduled appointments on time when you are relying on memory alone rather than referencing entries in a calendar. Kept up-to-date, calendars let you know where you need to be and when. They also make it easy to arrange appointments and avoid schedule conflicts. When you try to operate based on memory alone, you are playing a game you are likely to lose. Give yourself a better chance at winning throughout the week by writing down every meeting and appointment as you schedule it.

KEEPING A CALENDAR

If writing things down isn't your thing, there are many digital calendar options available. Smartphones come with a digital calendar app. Even with all the digital options on the market and the ability they afford for sharing with other people online, I recommend using a paper calendar for your household and keeping it in a place where everyone can see it on a daily basis. Our household actually has three calendars: one for me, one for my husband, and one for the whole family. As the children get older, they will likely start keeping their own calendars.

My calendar is a refillable binder that I call my "agenda book." For the eight-plus years that I have been using it, I've had to repair it a few times, but I like the way that it allows me to organize my calendar, my personal notes, my address book, and more. My husband uses a digital calendar for work, and our family calendar is made of paper and hangs on the refrigerator in our laundry room. This way, the kids have a chance to see, every day as they pass through the laundry room to get to the garage, exactly what we have going on throughout the week. I prefer a calendar that shows each month in its entirety. This is the style I grew up using, and it has stuck with me. I have tried using calendars that show only one week at a time, but I prefer being able to see, in a single glance, what is happening for the entire month. I customized a monthly calendar template I found online, and I print out a blank calendar for each month. You can find this template as a free printable on my website, www.livingjoydaily.com; simply type "printable calendar" in the search box.

I post our family's monthly calendar on the laundry room refrigerator inside a clear magnetic folder. This allows me to store multiple months' worth of calendar sheets there, with the current month displayed. (On my website, you will also find a link to an article that features the magnetic folder I use, in case you want to order one for yourself from Amazon.)

WHAT TO WRITE ON YOUR CALENDAR

It is pointless to keep a calendar unless you actually put it to use. Write down any and all upcoming appointments, important dates, and other pertinent information. I use our family calendar to keep track of the following details:

+ Doctor appointments

+ Dental appointments

+ Sports practices

+ Music lessons

+ Dance classes

+ Trips and vacations

+ Conferences

+ Out-of-town work trips

+ Birthdays and anniversaries

+ School theme days

+ School days off

CALENDARS AND BLOCK SCHEDULES: WHY USE BOTH?

As parents—the managers of our homes—we have a great deal to think about and keep track of on any given day. A calendar can help to clear our mental clutter because it frees us of the need to mentally remind ourselves of what we have going on that day, the next day, and the remainder of the week. We don't need to think about those things, because we have written them on our calendar as reminders.

The effort it takes to mentally anticipate everything that will be going on in your life during the week and month ahead can be stressful. I find that when I am not using my calendar and to-do lists as I should, I begin to feel frazzled. I also start to worry that some important events or tasks are being forgotten, or already have been. For me, writing things down is imperative. This practice helps to alleviate the stress and worry that I might forget something later.

 WRITING THINGS DOWN HELPS ALLEVIATE THE STRESS AND WORRY CAUSED BY TRYING TO REMEMBER EVERYTHING— AND FEARING YOU WILL FORGET SOMETHING IMPORTANT.

During especially busy times of the year, such as the months of November and December, you can experience even greater stress than usual if you are constantly trying to recall everything you need to accomplish, since the list it likely longer than your average list any other time of the year. It would be inconceivable for me to approach the holidays without my calendar and to-do list close by.

I do not record smaller tasks on my calendar. Instead, I keep a detailed daily agenda on a separate notepad, using the block scheduling method we previously discussed. This block schedule helps me to assess what I can reasonably expect to get done in a day. Putting all these details on my actual calendar would make my schedule seem too cluttered, not to mention taking up too much space. I like to use block scheduling one day at a time, while I depend on the calendar for reminding me of the most important upcoming appointments and events.

By maintaining a monthly calendar and making use of a daily block schedule, I create an organized plan of attack for each day. The calendar lists all upcoming appointments, and any pertinent information about those appointments gets written on the block schedule. The block schedule is made the day before, not weeks or months in advance. The calendar is used to keep track of appointments, meetings, and trips in the weeks and months to come. Therefore, these two tools each serve a unique purpose and are utilized in a different manner to fulfill that purpose.

FLEXIBILITY ABOVE ALL

As well-prepared as we may be, things still come up. We need to stay mentally prepared for unexpected events so that our schedules can have some flexibility. The school nurse may call and ask you to come pick up your sick child in the middle of the day. You may develop a toothache and need to see the dentist ASAP. Whatever it may be, prepare to shift things around on your schedule when new priorities suddenly arise.

If you plan so tight a schedule that every minute is divvied up according to a strict regimen, you are bound to become stressed and upset when something unexpectedly interrupts your schedule. Start each day with an awareness of what you have planned, but be ready to change directions and rearrange plans when necessary. Flexibility helps keep you sane and lets you accomplish things in their order of importance.

TO-DO LISTS

Another way to declutter your mind is to keep a running to-do list as a reference. From household tasks to personal phone calls to various errands, if I think of something that I need to do, I immediately write it down on my list. Otherwise, I will forget and later waste time trying to recall what it was that I needed to do.

Keeping a to-do list frees my mind to focus on whatever I am doing in the moment, because I don't have to continually remind myself of the things I need to take care of in the near future. Knowing that those items are written down gives me the freedom to focus on the present and the confidence that I won't forget about something important.

Right now, for example, I have the following items on my to-do list:

- Place a grocery store pickup order

- Install wire fence in garden to keep out rabbits

- Order replacement cushions for patio chairs

- Clean chicken coop

- Watch YouTube videos on haircutting techniques

- Respond to email from Jessy about video teachings

- Return storage bins to attic

- Use paint to touch up area in front of stools in the kitchen

- Clean outdoor patio pillows

- Send a birthday present to Lydia (my niece)

- Weed the backyard

- Start Brielle with her online piano lessons

All these items are tasks that need to be done soon but are not as pressing or important as feeding my family dinner or doing our daily homeschooling. I must work these additional items into my schedule throughout the week. Therefore, I use block scheduling, in conjunction with my calendar and to-do list, to weave it all together.

I like to use a medium-sized yellow notepad for my block scheduling and a spiral-bound journaling book for my to-do lists, so they are easy enough to carry along with me wherever I go. I also use my to-do list journal for recording notes during meetings and appointments. I prefer hardcover journaling books because they stay closed and prevent their contents from getting wrinkled inside my carryall bag. The yellow notepad, on the other hand, typically gets tucked inside my agenda book. Every evening, I create my block schedule for the next day, consulting the to-do list in my journaling book and determining which tasks will fit into which blocks.

There is a good reason why I use three different items instead of a single book for keeping track of all these details. I use the calendar, the yellow notepad, and the journaling book together, but, because they are separate, I can lay them out side-by-side for the sake of comparison. Keeping every detail in my agenda book would make it impossible for me to view everything at the same time (since those details would be on different pages) and would make the effort of creating a block schedule far more time-consuming, because I would constantly be flipping back and forth between different pages.

At the end of each day, I check the to-do list in my journal book and cross off every item I completed. There is great satisfaction in checking off items from your to-do list. There are times when I need to begin a new page for my to-do list, and there are still a few items remaining on the existing list. In this case, I begin the new list with those remaining items, so that they have priority, before tearing out the old page. Some weeks, I use just one page—the same to-do list—for all seven days. At other times, when life is more hectic, I may work through several pages of to-do lists in one week. How could I ever expect to complete a list of thirty items in one week if I didn't write them down? I would never remember them! Keeping a running to-do list is such a helpful mental reminder. It also gives me the ability to distribute those items in the block schedule I make every night.

AN EXTRA TIP: USE A CARRYALL BAG

I rarely go anywhere without my carryall bag. For some of you, your "carryall" may be a briefcase. For others, it may be a diaper bag or a big purse. I use a carryall bag because it works well for my current phase of life and allows me to be prepared for whatever I have planned on any given day. That's because anything I know I'll need, I put in the bag and take with me when I leave the house in the morning. That includes a smaller purse that fits inside the carryall bag, making it possible for me to grab just the purse and take it inside when I go shopping, for example. I also take along my makeup bag, a small bottle of hand sanitizer, my agenda book, my to-do list, my journaling book, and a pair of flat shoes (since I usually leave the house wearing heels but can stand to wear those for only so long). If I am going to be gone for most of the day with appointments and such, I will likely pack a few snacks and canned beverages, such as V8 +Energy drinks. (In my experience, cans are less likely to leak than screw-top bottles.)

Using a carryall bag every day makes it easy for me to pack, the night before, what I will need the following day. When I lay out my clothes, I look at my agenda and see what I have scheduled so I can select an outfit accordingly and can place any extra items—whether accessories or something else—in the carryall bag.

Let's say that one of the items on my to-do list is to write thank-you notes for the various Christmas presents I received. As I'm preparing my carryall bag, I will pack some stationery and a nice pen, so that I can get started on the notes if I find myself with time to spare. We all have spare moments throughout the day just waiting to be put to use. The question is, how are we using that time? Many of us—myself included—easily default to doing mindless activities on our smartphones. But if we've set limits for ourselves on phone use, and if we come prepared with a carryall bag full of supplies for the various items on our to-do list, we can optimize our free time. If we don't plan ahead, then we will end up wasting time. Planning ahead and predetermining how we will spend the time between our daily appointments is how we combat idleness and maximize productivity.

TAKE CHARGE OF YOUR HEALTH AND ENERGY

I wrote this extra chapter for anyone who is following the advice I've shared in this book but finds they lack the energy to follow through. If you are having problems getting things done because you are too tired or don't have enough energy, then you need to take a look at your overall health, with a special focus on exercise and nutrition. The food we put into our bodies should be thought of as fuel. We may have heard this concept enough times, but have we internalized it? I have struggled with this mindset myself.

DIET

There have been periods of my life when I ate fast-food meals just about every other day. I could stay healthy-looking (not overweight) because, many days, that fast-food meal was my only true meal. My entire daily intake of calories would be consumed in a single "meal" of preservative-laden junk food. I could stay thin enough with this habit by counting calories, but I was not fueling my body with the proper nutrients. It took me far too many years to realize that being thin is not the same as being healthy.

My perspective on food changed significantly when I started looking at food as fuel for my body. Food can be enjoyable, but we should center our dietary decisions based more on what our bodies *need* than what our minds *want* us to enjoy eating. I am not going to prescribe a dietary plan for you. I may have earned an associate's degree in fitness and nutrition, but that does not make me a high-level nutrition expert. However, I know enough to understand that healthy eating affects the way you feel and function as a human being. It is not about looking a certain way, because we can deceive ourselves into thinking we are healthy simply because we are not obese. It is about making wise decisions for the long term, because our eating habits and our lifestyle—whether active or sedentary—will eventually catch up with us, possibly when it's too late to make changes that will improve or prolong our lives.

Feeding yourself fuel rather than empty calories is very important. When you fuel your body properly, with the right nutrients, you have more energy, and you feel better overall.

Taking care of medical issues that come up due to poor eating habits and a lack of exercise can be time-consuming. You can eat up literally years of your life fighting off ailments or disease because of bad life-style choices. It is up to you to make choices that will benefit your body. Certainly, some diseases and ailments are not preventable. But there are a great many that are tied to the way we have cared for our bodies. Try to make healthy choices and to incorporate exercise into your daily routine. You won't regret it!

EXERCISE

Exercise is important for the body and mind alike. By exercising regularly, you boost your energy level. How is that possible? Because exercising increases your metabolism and strengthens your heart. According to the Mayo Clinic, exercise raises your energy level:

Winded by grocery shopping or household chores? Regular physical activity can improve your muscle strength and boost your endurance.

Exercise delivers oxygen and nutrients to your tissues and helps your cardiovascular system work more efficiently. And when your heart and lung health improve, you have more energy to tackle daily chores.[4]

Exercise is also a known endorphin booster, helping us to feel ener-gized and able to do more during the day. As you exercise on a regular basis, you will find that this endorphin release occurs more frequently, helping to increase your overall energy level.

The benefits of exercise have been proven by scientists to improve both your health and your mental well-being. Just think of how much you could accomplish in a day if you had more energy!

4. Mayo Clinic Staff, "Exercise: 7 benefits of regular physical activity," 11 May 2019, https://www.mayoclinic.org/healthy-lifestyle/fitness/in-depth/exercise/art-20048389.

If you have trouble focusing, then take a walk, go for a run, or try a different form of cardiovascular exercise. Get your body working, and your brain will focus better, because exercise increases the oxygen level in your bloodstream.

VITAMINS

Many of us are deficient in our intake of certain vitamins because our diets alone do not give us a high enough concentration of them. Most doctors suggest taking a daily multivitamin and/or other vitamin supplements to boost overall health and well-being. Talk to your doctor about your diet, and discuss whether a multivitamin or another type of supplement might be helpful.

Vitamins also equip our bodies to fight off the viruses and illnesses that can stall our productivity temporarily or in the long term. Even if you are exposed to a virus, your body will be better prepared to fight back if you have a strong immune system. Some essential vitamins that are linked to a strengthened immune system, according to the Cleveland Clinic, are vitamins C, E, A, and D; folic acid; iron; selenium; and zinc.[5] It is recommended that you get these vitamins and nutrients through your diet rather than primarily from supplements, if possible. There are some vitamins that the Cleveland Clinic recommends never taking as a supplement, such as vitamin E, as it can be dangerous when taken incorrectly. Vitamin E in a supplement can be dangerous, as it *may* cause an increased risk of prostate cancer, according to the Mayo Clinic[6].

Eating foods that are rich in the vitamins and nutrients listed above can help you strengthen your immune system. If you do feel that your diet alone is not giving you all the vitamins and nutrients that you need,

5. Cleveland Clinic, "8 Vitamins & Minerals You Need for a Healthy Immune System," 4 December 2020, https://health.clevelandclinic.org/eat-these-foods-to-boost-your-immune-system/.
6. Mayo Clinic Staff, "Vitamin E," 13 November 2020, https://www.mayoclinic.org/drugs-supplements-vitamin-e/art-20364144.

talk to your doctor. Always consult your physician before starting a vitamin or supplement regimen.

UNDERLYING HEALTH ISSUES

If you are eating right, exercising, and getting the right vitamins and nutrients to fuel your body—and you *still* feel that you are lacking energy—then you may need to consult your doctor. There are certain conditions, such as thyroid dysfunction and various autoimmune disorders, that can cause energy levels to dip below normal, resulting in lethargy. Consult your doctor if you question your energy levels and are looking for more answers. You can Google symptoms and treatments all you want, but any decisions about your health are best left to someone who can examine you in person. Be your own advocate, but also go to the experts (in person) for authoritative answers you can trust. Google can be helpful for certain things, but please don't depend on it for guidance regarding your health decisions.

COMBATTING EXHAUSTION AND BURNOUT

Do you get to the end of the day feeling physically exhausted? If so, join the club! Feeling worn out or exhausted at the end of the day is not a new phenomenon to parenting or running a household. Raising kids is hard. The daily demands of care and effort can be downright exhausting.

Make sure that you are giving yourself enough downtime during the week to unwind and regroup. You can't keep going like the Energizer Bunny if you aren't getting refueled and refreshed. We refuel with food and sleep, but our emotional well-being is often refreshed by acts of "self-care." Treating ourselves to some downtime is not an act of selfishness, nor does it mean we are being negligent and shirking our family responsibilities in exchange for "me time." Work out the details of your downtime with your partner or spouse so that you both get the relaxation you need.

 TREATING OURSELVES TO SOME DOWNTIME IS NOT AN ACT OF SELFISHNESS, NOR DOES IT MEAN WE ARE BEING NEGLIGENT AND SHIRKING OUR FAMILY RESPONSIBILITIES IN EXCHANGE FOR "ME TIME."

Self-care looks different for everyone. For many of my friends, it means getting a massage, going to the gym, or having their hair or nails done at a salon. Personally, I am refreshed after working in the garden, listening to an audiobook, or spending time with my friends from book club. Focusing on my relationship with God by doing daily devotionals also helps me feel centered and energized. Figure out what it is that refreshes you so that you can plan it into your schedule, whether daily, weekly, or monthly. Yes, put it on the schedule, because, in our hectic lives, downtime and self-care often come last. If we don't make it a point to schedule some downtime for ourselves, we are likely to keep on working and going and doing until we reach a breaking point.

Exhaustion at the end of the day, if it's accompanied by a sense of fulfillment and accomplishment, can be a rewarding feeling. However, if you are not taking care of yourself in the process, you may exhaust yourself to a point of breakdown. Physical exhaustion without any pauses for self-care can lead to emotional and mental burnout. You need to be sure to take care of yourself so that you can keep taking care of the ones you love. You are worth it, and your family will thank you, because you come back refreshed and in a better emotional state to continue doing life with them.

REMEMBER, YOU ARE WORTHY

There is only one you. You are worth every investment of time and effort into your own well-being. God created you for a purpose in this world. It may be your career, raising a family, and/or another special purpose that God has placed on your heart. Your mission and purpose cannot be completed unless you are healthy enough to fulfill it. Make sure you take care of yourself so that you can use your time to do what you need to do. Time is fleeting, but so is our health. Do your best to care for yourself, so that you have the time to do what you need to do to complete your life's purpose. If you want to be around to enjoy your grandchildren—and, Lord willing, your great-children—take care of yourself now. You matter, and there is only one you.

ABOUT THE AUTHOR

D r. Magdalena Battles is a writer and conference speaker whose specialties include parenting, child development, family relationships, domestic violence, and sexual assault. She shares her real-life experiences and professional insights on her website, LivingJoyDaily.com, and on Lifehack.org, where she was named one of their top writers. She is also the author of *Let Them Play: The Importance of Play and 100 Child Development Activities* and *6 Hidden Behaviors That Destroy Families: Strategies for Healthier and More Loving Relationships*.

Dr. Battles earned a bachelor's degree in child psychology and a master's degree in professional counseling, both from Liberty University, and a doctorate in clinical and academic psychology from Walden University. She has also completed postgraduate studies on "Technologies in Education" at Harvard University.

While she may seem all business, in her spare time, Dr. Battles enjoys camping with her family, visiting national parks, reading books, decorating, organizing, shopping, incubating and raising Silkie chickens, and spending time with extended family. She is also an active volunteer in her community and church. Dr. Battles and her husband, Justin, reside in Texas with their daughter, Brielle; their twin boys, Alex and Charlie; a dog named Max; and a handful of Silkie chickens.

http://www.LivingJoyDaily.com

https://www.facebook.com/groups/DrMagdalenaBattles/

https://www.lifehack.org/author/dr-magdalena-battles

Welcome to Our House!

We Have a Special Gift for You

It is our privilege and pleasure to share in your love of Christian books. We are committed to bringing you authors and books that feed, challenge, and enrich your faith.

To show our appreciation, we invite you to sign up to receive a specially selected **Reader Appreciation Gift**, with our compliments. Just go to the Web address at the bottom of this page.

God bless you as you seek a deeper walk with Him!

WE HAVE A GIFT FOR YOU. VISIT:

whpub.me/nonfictionthx

WHITAKER
HOUSE